Praise for The Executive Coach Approach to Marketing

Pomerantz and Brodie have written a book that every executive coach needs about what most executive coaches don't know – how to market your coaching! The Executive Coach Approach to Marketing is a crucial read for anyone who wants to be a successful executive coach!

Marshall Goldsmith
International best-selling author or editor of 35 books
including the #1 New York Times bestseller – Triggers

So many coaches engage in magical thinking about marketing and building their practice – help is really needed. This is the one book that really covers all the bases, using true coaching tools to help the coach help himself. Those who commit to Pomerantz and Brodie's engaging and exhaustive approach will not only be turning clients away, they will become better coaches as well.

Madeleine Homan Blanchard
MCC, Co-Founder and Director of Coaching Services, The Ken Blanchard Companies,
Co-author of Coaching in Organizations and Leverage Your Best

Have you ever wondered how some executive coaches are able to authentically sell their services to senior leaders in organizations all over the world? This book pulls back the curtain on two master coaches with proven track records to reveal to you exactly how to do it for yourself; from mindsets to a menu of marketing actions you can try. Save time and get profitable faster with this golden guide.

Dr. C. Jeannine Sandstrom
CEO, CoachWorks International Inc., Author of Legacy Leadership

Yes! Finally a "How-To" book to support coaches in marketing their business which is actually useful! Easy to read - Easy to follow - Offering specific steps supported by a toolbox of information at every turn. Eliminate the other books from your shelf, incorporate this one, and you will be off on your successful coaching business journey!

Bobette Reeder
M.Ed., MCC, President of Reeder Coaching Group
Co-Founder and Founding President, The Coach Initiative

If you're like many coaches, you might feel a bit uncomfortable marketing and selling your coaching services to organizations. With this book, Brodie and Pomerantz offer great advice, tools and techniques to help you, genuinely and congruently, grow your business. These seasoned and successful coaches and business leaders provide you with a roadmap that guides you through a COACH approach to offering your coaching services - an approach that uses what you're best at - your relationship skills. I can't recommend this highly enough!

Terrie Lupberger
Executive Coach, Author and Advisor to C-Suites and Teams
former CEO of Newfield Network

Lots of people offer business development advice for coaches, but most of them are not seasoned coaches who have built a successful practice with delighted clients. Suzi and Ian are the real deal and know exactly what it takes to attract and keep clients. Even better, they show you how to do this naturally, using strengths that you already have as a coach.

Andrew Neitlich
Director, Center for Executive Coaching
Author of Guerrilla Marketing for Coaches

If only I'd had this book when I started out! Packed with practical tools and strategies, it will help you grow your business so you can make the impact that inspired you to begin with. It's a no-brainer investment!

Margie Warrell
Women's Leadership Coach
Bestselling Author of Stop Playing Safe and Find Your Courage

The Executive Coach Approach to Marketing is a treasure trove of tried and true tools for defining and successfully growing your business as a coach. This book gives everyone – from early stage to master level coaches – valuable insights, critical questions, and proven processes that will focus your marketing and accelerate your business success.

Steve Lishansky
CEO of Optimize International
Founder and Executive Director of the Executive Coaching Institute

The Executive Coach Approach
To Marketing

The Executive Coach Approach To Marketing

USE YOUR COACHING STRENGTHS TO WIN YOUR IDEAL CLIENTS AND PAINLESSLY GROW YOUR BUSINESS

Suzi Pomerantz and Ian Brodie

ISBN-13: 9780992763190
ISBN-10: 0992763193
Published by Rainmaker Publishing

Dedication

To all those leaders who strive to make their businesses and the world a better place, and to the coaches who support them in doing so!

Table of Contents

How to Get the Most from This Book

You are an executive coach. Or maybe you're a leadership coach. Or a business coach. Whatever you call yourself, you are doing the work of supporting executives and leaders to achieve their greatest possible results. And you want to do more coaching, with more leaders, and have more impact. You also would like to make a consistent and predictable six-figure (or more) income while you're at it. Right?

That's why we created this executive coach approach to marketing your coaching services.

Who Is This Book For?

First, here's who it's NOT for. This is not about how to sell giant, mega speaking or training programs and have other people working for you to "coach" your content. Nor is it for those who want to turn your knowledge into products and retire from doing the work of coaching.

This is for you if you have a *passion for coaching* and want to sell your coaching services to executives in organizations. It is for the coach who loves coaching one-to-one and wants more of that. This book is for the tens of thousands of coaches around the world who want to crack the code on how to sell executive coaching services and grow a coaching business without selling your soul or growing more gray hairs.

Purpose

Our purpose in writing this book is to share what we've dubbed "the coach approach" to selling leadership or executive coaching services - in other words, the most direct route to getting paying coaching clients. In the book, we will mention other methods, but the real route to getting your ideal 1:1 executive coaching clients is by talking to them, not by hiding behind social media, your website, or other marketing tools. We teach a personal, relationship-based approach to marketing and selling using your coaching skills. There are many programs on the market for coaches by well-meaning marketing experts claiming to have THE system or THE approach that when you pay them thousands of dollars to learn it, will catapult you to six-figure success. Buyer beware! The market is flooded with entrepreneurs who are making a fortune by selling a money-making scheme to coaches. That's not us. We're just two master executive coaches who have successfully grown our respective coaching businesses for well over twenty years each, and we got together to discuss what works, and what doesn't.

The style of this book is a dialogue between two expert coaches on two different continents, chatting about how to get executive and organizational leader clients in the quickest, most direct, and most effective way. We are both twenty-plus year veterans in the field, and you'll get each of our perspectives. We discovered in our dialogues that we agree on the core principles, not always on all the details and approaches, but you'll get it all here, with lots of options, so you can choose what resonates with you.

How to Get the Most Out of This Book

This book is for all levels of coach, whether you have an existing network of potential clients or are starting from scratch.

Chances are, you're one of these:

- **Thinking about becoming a coach** - For now just skim the chapters to understand what you'll have to do at each stage so you'll understand what's coming, but pay special attention to the chapter on building your network now, before you need it! Use the informational interview approach to determine if coaching is right for you - how you'd like to coach and where. Be sure to talk to experienced coaches and check your assumptions as you set up your business.
- **Newly trained coach** - Go through the book step by step and pay special attention to the fundamentals as well as the early chapters on building your contact network. If you do find yourself in a sales meeting, skip ahead to that part of the book, so you'll know how to land the client!
- **First year of coaching** - Do all the exercises, use all the tools in the book, and seek to continually tweak and adjust your business based on the results

you're seeing. Look at the Bowtie Model and track your numbers on that. Then review it quarterly to see if you're getting enough people into your system to guide you on where to focus to maximize your results.

- **Established coach** - Review the book regularly, especially if you find yourself in a slow season with fewer clients than you'd like to have. Analyze your current habits to determine if your groove has become a rut, and recalibrate accordingly.

- **Seasoned master coach** - Your goal may well be to raise your fee levels and work with higher-level clients in more lucrative organizations. So review the segments on how to build sustainability in your business, building clients while billing time. And, of course, make sure you continue to excel at the fundamentals.

Download the workbook to get the most from the book so you can work on the exercises actively and apply them immediately in your business. The exercise questions are all included in this book, but coaches tell us they love having all the exercises collected together in one place with space to write, which is just what the workbook provides. You can access the workbook for free and download your own printable copy of workbook from The Library of Professional Coaching here: http://libraryof-professionalcoaching.com/marketing/executive-coach-marketing-resource-centre/

Keep coming back to the book, with sticky notes at hand. Try things out and revisit the book regularly to pick up extra skills and resources to take your results to higher levels. You'll catch something new each time you read it. We've also heard from early readers who recommend that you get a study buddy or set up a small learning circle to discuss and apply the elements presented here.

Who We Are

We are both seasoned master coaches who have been coaching executives and leaders in hundreds of organizations around the world. We partnered for your benefit, since so many coaches ask us regularly how we do what we do.

So first to introduce ourselves: I'm Suzi Pomerantz. I've been helping executives and teams find clarity in chaos for over twenty-three years now. I've held the ICF Master Coach credential for over seventeen years. I've coached leaders in more than 200 organizations worldwide, and I've started or co-founded a number of organizations in the coaching world, such as the International Consortium for Coaching in

Organizations, the Leading Coaching Center, and the Library of Professional Coaching. I also teach at the College of Executive Coaching and I have a few books out, one of which is the best-selling book about business development called *Seal the Deal*. The *Harvard Business Review* invited me to serve on their advisory board, and my full-time business is coaching executives and leaders as the CEO of Innovative Leadership International LLC. On a personal note, I live with my husband and two children just outside of Washington, D.C.

And I'm Ian Brodie, a marketing specialist focused on helping coaches and other professionals to attract and win more clients. In my time as a coach and a consultant myself, I've sold multimillion dollar engagements around the world and worked in seventeen different countries. *Top Sales World Magazine* listed me as one of the top fifty global thought leaders in marketing and sales, OpenView Labs say I'm one of the top sales influencers in the world, and RainToday named my website as one of the "resources of the decade" for professional services marketing. I came to coaching from a consulting background as I started to work with more senior clients, and I became known for being able to sell to and engage with "tricky" clients. When I set up my own practice, I discovered just how challenging and different things can be for sole practitioner coaches without the support of a larger organization, so my recent work has all been about sharing what really works for coaches' marketing at a very practical level.

I live in Cheshire in the UK with my wife and two sons, and these days work virtually with clients all around the world.

Our Promise

As your leaders in this process, we're both committed to helping you understand the psychology behind selling coaching services to executives and how to find the right executives while leveraging your coaching strengths to turn executive prospects into paying clients - without being salesy or pushy or anything other than who you naturally are as a brilliant coach.

This book details a robust program that expands and builds upon what we initially developed as a part of a year-long, live and online program for executive coaches worldwide. It will show you how to get corporate clients or complex organizational clients in a system that's easy, fast, sustainable, comfortable, and recognizable to you as a coach. That means we won't be using the language of information marketers or sales experts, but we'll be pointing out the *coach approach* to each of the core business development areas we're covering so that you can simply focus on how to get comfortable with doing what it takes to get more executive coaching clients consistently.

We show coaches how to find and naturally connect with more potential clients and how to comfortably turn them into paying clients - in particular, how to do it quickly and easily without feeling like an aggressive salesperson. You'll learn how to sell coaching services congruently with who you are as a coach.

Take a few moments to respond to the questions in the Coach Approach Quiz below to have a baseline for your growth as you progress through the book.

Coach Approach Quiz

As you know, gaining clarity prior to beginning about your intended outcomes can be the difference between a successful coaching program and a mediocre one. In that vein, we'd like to assist your thinking and ensure that you are clear before you embark upon the rest of the book. Please respond to the questions below and be sure to note the date for yourself. Consider it a journal entry to kick off your readiness to learn the coach approach!

1. How long have you had your coaching business?
2. What are your top strengths as a coach?
3. Who do you coach?
4. What are the top challenges your clients face that you help them solve?
5. Where are your ideal clients based?
6. How would you rate your current success at marketing and bringing in new clients?
7. What's the biggest thing you struggle with in networking, marketing, and sales?
8. What do you hope to get out of this book?
9. Where do you hope to see your business in a year's time?
10. In what ways are you hoping this learning journey will be different from everything you've done prior to now?
11. What will you do to sustain your learning over time?
12. How will you incorporate your chapter-by-chapter learning into your day-to-day business operations?

CHAPTER 1

The Coach Approach: An Overview of Business Development

Suzi: This is your starting point for the core system, and the materials we will cover here are a direct result of polls and focus groups we conducted with hundreds of executive coaches worldwide. The vast majority of the data that we found revealed that what you want and need most is to find and connect with more potential clients and to have a quick and comfortable system for turning them into paying clients.

We will provide you with tools you can immediately take action on so that you will gain value; it will be practical and easy to apply rather than theoretical or cerebral. We will dive into mindsets and foundational principles as well as tactical, practical, and transactional nuts and bolts for getting your executive coaching business to consistently yield the financial results you want. We are going to walk you step by step through how to find and connect to more of your ideal potential clients and how to turn them into paying clients as quickly and easily as possible.

As a reminder, if you haven't already done the Coach Approach Quiz, please take a moment to do that before you move on.

Chapters 1–5 comprise content and exercises across four topics:

- A look at the buyers of executive coaching and what executives look for in a coach.
- The various options for finding potential clients.
- The core coach approach to finding clients.

- Methods for using the coach approach to find the clients you're looking for.
  - o We're going to cover prospecting, targeting, whether or not to have a niche, and how to find and connect with those who are open to purchasing executive coaching services from you.

Ian: This chapter sets the stage for the full suite of materials we will be giving you, including all the practical actionable information and road maps that you need to find potential clients and connect with them in meaningful ways, and to help potential clients to decide if they want to be clients, converting them to clients, and the proven methods to systematically and sustainably grow your executive coaching business, all using the coach approach especially designed to work with your comfort zone and get you real results fast.

Business development is a system and process that you will of course customize to your own style, personality, values, and needs, but regardless of how you customize it, the most critical aspect of business development is creating a pipeline of activity to be continually moving people through. For that reason, this first chapter is the most critical because without the ability to continually find people for each of the various stages of the pipeline into your business, your results will be spotty at best.

The biggest challenge most coaches face is not putting enough people into their system up front and throughout. It's not so much that they lack the hustle or the mindset of continual action, it's that they don't necessarily understand the scope of the numbers involved. The number of people it takes to keep refreshing your pipeline when some people will move faster at stages and others will move more slowly is much higher than you imagine. But don't worry: We're going to help you get there.

Suzi: So first, it's important to understand the big picture. This Bowtie Model© is from my book *Seal the Deal*, and it provides an overview of the business development cycle as an integrated model of both the sales cycle and the service cycle. It reads left to right, starting with the whole vast universe of potential users of your executive coaching services. We will be going into depth with this model in a later chapter when we look at the coach approach to sealing the deal. However, for now, it's useful to know that not all the potential users of your services will actually be in your business development process, which is why this first chapter on how to find folks to bring into the process is critical.

The Bowtie Model

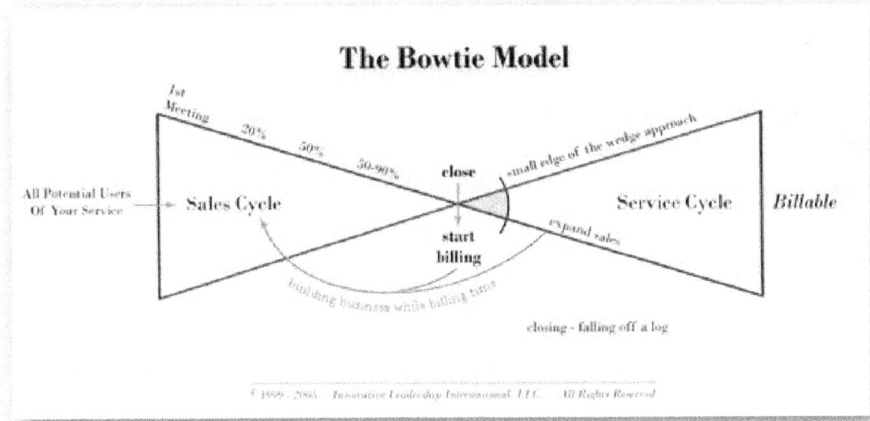

Moving from left to right across the Bowtie Model©, if you imagine that you meet a hundred people, you can, in general, expect ten of them to be appropriate potential clients. You will move them through the process, and can reasonably expect one to two of those ten to become clients and move with you into the service side of the diagram. These numbers become a bit daunting if it's a pure numbers game, but the coach approach is more strategic than that. You need not meet with a hundred random people if you can be more strategic and targeted about who you're meeting, making the picture more digestible. You may only need to meet twenty targeted, strategically identified people to find one to two clients.

Of course, you'd probably like to find more than one or two clients for your business. So first it's important to figure out how much money you want to make in a given year. Based on your current rate, how many clients do you need to sign up, taking into account the average life cycle of your clients? We're not saying here that you have to price based on a single rate, because there are many different ways of pricing. Start modeling your numbers using the single rate calculation...you can always re-work the modeling for other pricing structures in the future. In order to make this calculation, use your average current rate for working with clients, or make one up for the sake of the exercise if you haven't yet established your pricing, or if you're considering raising your rates.

Next, determine how many new clients you need in a month in order to hit those targets. Then, using the Bowtie Model© and using the numbers that are relevant for your particular business, how many potential clients do you need to go and find each month in order to move them through your Bowtie Model© and seal the deal with the number of clients you need each month?

For example, let say you want to make $200,000 dollars per year starting in January. Suppose you charge $10,000 dollars per executive for a six-month engagement. To make the amount you want to make, you'll need twenty clients, all of whom would need to start prior to June or pay in advance when they do start. Depending on your specific numbers and the way you do your client acquisition, you'll need to meet anywhere from 400 to 2,000 potential users of your services, depending on how strategic you are in your target market, in order to get twenty of them all the way through your sales cycle and into the service side, meaning they become paying clients.

Ian: This is where we come in. If you're not currently out there meeting literally hundreds of people regularly and you don't feel comfortable doing that, you're in the right place and we're going to help you get moving. Our assumptions are that you're already trained as an executive coach, you've already launched your business, and you're eager to grow it beyond what you've already established, meaning you'd like more one-to-one executive clients coming to you for coaching services and you've got room in your book of business to add a few more relevant clients.

We assume also that you are similar to the folks we heard from in our polls and focus group, which revealed that the number-one obstacle was not feeling comfortable marketing or selling. Our assumption is that you wouldn't want us teaching business development in terms of sales language like targeting, pipelines, prospecting, lead generation, enrollment conversions, and other sales terminologies, so we've written this book in plain English with a sprinkling of coach jargon, but we keep the sales and corporate lingo to a minimum.

Below you'll find a checklist for action to help you envision your business and where you'd like to take it. You'll also find tools to allow you to think about your own business in the context of the Bowtie Model©. Once you've done that, we'll move on to the next topics.

Toolbox!

Checklist for Action: Envisioning Your Business

Use the Bowtie Model© to Understand and Plot YOUR Sales-into-Service Cycle

Checklist for Action: Envisioning Your Business

Use this action checklist to think through and envision your coaching business and map out your plan forward.

1. Clarify your vision: What do you want (ideal state)?
2. Identify where you are now: What is the current state of your business situation?
3. What is your current level of activity with regard to business development in each area of networking, marketing, and sales?
4. Identify what you need to do to build a bridge from where you are now to where you want to be. What will it take?
5. Identify your core values and the core values of your company.
6. List the core competencies for you and your company.
7. Determine your product and service offerings.
8. Research the product and service offerings of your closest competitors in the market.
9. Ideal Client Profiling: Determine with whom you want to work and map out a profile of the ideal.
10. Revisit your business plan or write one.

Use the Bowtie Model© to Understand and Plot YOUR Sales-into-Service Cycle

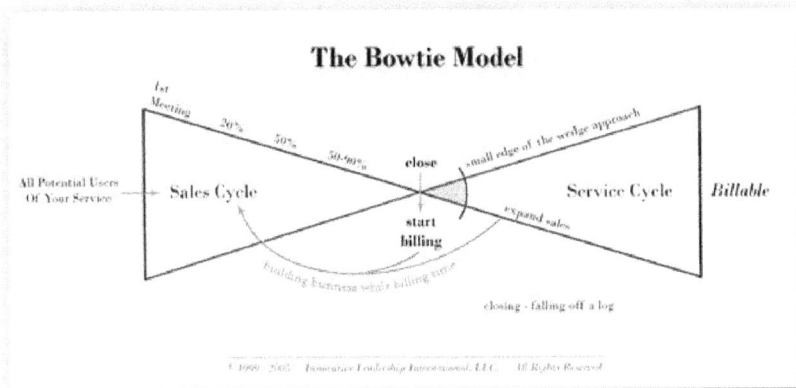

The Bowtie Model

Critical to your success in marketing your services to executive clients is understanding your personal sales cycle; i.e., how long it takes you to go from when you first learn about a potential client (whether through referral, networking, inbound request, or your own outreach efforts) and when the work begins (meaning you have an agreement in place and they're paying you). Use the Bowtie Model and the chart below for either planning or tracking purposes, or both!

Planning: Use the Bowtie Model© above with the chart below for planning purposes by inputting historical data from your own experience to determine the length of your own sales cycle. Start by listing all your current clients in the "potential buyer" column. List the dates of your meetings with them so that you can see how long your sales process typically takes. You can then estimate how many meetings you need to get a client, so that you can calculate how many initial contacts you'll need in order to get as many clients as you'd ultimately like to have at any time.

Tracking: You can use the chart below for ongoing tracking purposes by listing names as you meet people in real time, keeping yourself on track with the process so that you can manage your client growth against your intentions for your business. It's particularly helpful to track once you have many contacts in the sales process with you so that you will always know where you are in the process or what your next step should be.

Name of Potential Buyer	Date of 1st Meeting	Date of 2nd Meeting	3rd Meeting or Proposal or Alternate Next Steps	How Many Meetings Before Work Begins?	Over What Period of Time?

Meeting Tracker

Use the Bowtie Model© to Set Your Targets

Capture your findings: Analyze your chart using the Bowtie Model and either using your completed planning sheet of current clients or by using estimates, answer the following questions to give you an idea of how many contacts and meetings you will need over how long a time period to meet your goals.

How many meetings does it take to move someone from initial contact to potential buyer to client?
How long does that typically take (days, weeks, months, years)?
Setting your targets: Answer the following questions to help set your targets.

1.   How much money would you like to make in a year?

2.   What is your current rate and how long do clients coach with you?

3.   Based on the answers to the questions above, how many clients do you need to bring on board in a year?

4.   How many new clients would that be per month?

5.   Using the Bowtie Model, how many new targeted people (potential clients) do you need to go find each month in order to move them through your Bowtie Model to get to the number of clients you need per month?

CHAPTER 2
The Client Perspective

I an: In this chapter we're going to look at what executives look for when they're thinking of hiring a coach. Although every executive is different, they share many common needs and concerns when it comes to hiring coaches. We're going to look at some of those common factors as well as how you can develop an in-depth picture of what your specific ideal clients want and need to be ready to hire you.

Suzi: The better you understand what your potential clients are looking for when they're thinking of hiring a coach, the easier it's going to be for you to find the right executive clients. But this knowledge will also help you better present yourself in a way that they see you're meeting their needs and delivering the results they're looking for. Knowing your clients' perspectives goes deeper than that.

Ian: Your understanding of your potential clients, who they are, what goes on in their day-to-day work, the challenges they have, and their goals and aspirations, all comes across in every interaction you have with them. Every time you speak to a potential client or they visit your website or even when they hear things about you from others, it sends a message about whether you "get" them, whether you understand their specific situation, and how comfortable they would feel working with you.

That deep understanding of your clients also helps you coach them better. If you speak the same language as your clients, it's much easier to get down to work. If your client has to explain to you what they mean half the time, it becomes a frustrating and difficult experience for them and your coaching won't be as effective.

The Buyers' Perspective - What Executives Are Looking For
Suzi: First, we need to look at the primary buyers of executive coaching in organizations and the people who influence those buying decisions. Then we'll look at,

generically, the big things your buyers are looking for. Yes, every potential client is different, but there are some key common factors that ever executive looks for. We'll show you how to build your ideal client profile. From that you'll be able to identify some more specific things that your buyers in particular are looking for. Finally, we'll cover some of the most frequently asked questions that executive coaches have about understanding potential clients. Things like, what happens if you haven't got much experience yet or what do you do if they don't know what they want?

So who actually buys executive coaching? You probably know from your own experience that there are three, sometimes four, types of people involved in hiring an executive coach. Ideal is when the executive makes the hiring decision directly, and an ICF study from a few years ago revealed that about two-thirds of the time the client you'll actually be working with is the hiring decision-maker. Other instances are a mixed bag. Sometimes a more senior executive will appoint a coach for someone on their team and sometimes, when an organization is buying a coaching program for a group of leaders rather than hiring a coach for one specific person, the human resources vice president or head of learning and development will take the lead.

In general, the person you need to understand best is the executive you're going to be coaching. But even then, when the executive is making the hiring decision, chances are that they may check it out with another executive, perhaps the CEO (if they are not the CEO). There may also be some corporate HR rules about certifications or who is approved to do this type of personal development and how it has to be processed through their procurement system. In most organizations, major purchases and sometimes quite small ones have to run through an internal procurement system, so that means you may have to deal with a procurement official as well. Even if you deal primarily with the situation in which the executive you're working with is the sole decision maker, it's still wise to understand who the other stakeholders are, what they are looking for, as well as their indicators of success. When you know you're in a complex buying process, it's also critical to know the relationships between those different stakeholders and how they influence each other. Systems theory applies to organizations and is relevant to keep in mind during the marketing and sales process.

We'll be covering in depth in a later segment of this book how you help your clients decide if they're ready to buy coaching, but for now let's just focus on the senior executives who are your potential clients and what they are looking for from a coach.

Ian: Executives are generally looking to hire an executive coach out of a desire to improve performance. That could have to do with leadership, communication, motivation, or managing their team, but it also could be related to anything that's holding them back from being effective. You may end up working with them on time management or even on some personal issues that are overflowing into their work. That is part of what makes this job so interesting - the variety of issues you can end up being hired to help executives address.

In 2009 the ICF asked coaching clients for the most important reasons they hired a coach. Here are the top responses from the 1,000+ executives who responded to the survey:

1. Business management (with 36 percent putting it in their top three reasons)
2. Self-esteem or self-confidence (33 percent)
3. Career opportunities (31 percent)
4. Work-life balance (29 percent)
5. Work performance (29 percent)

Other reasons included communication skills, team effectiveness, interpersonal skills and relationships, and quite a mixed set of issues ranging from hard skills to soft skills to psychology, but none of them dominant.

This reveals a critical fact to keep in mind: there isn't one single issue that executives hire coaches to help them with. That doesn't mean you couldn't specialize in one of these areas and have enough clients to keep you busy for a long, long time. But it does mean that you shouldn't assume that all potential clients have the same exact needs. It means that in your marketing, they need to see that you're able to work across a variety of areas to help them achieve their goals.

So what are they looking for from a coach?

Suzi: The same ICF study with executive coaching clients shows that there's diversity in what clients are looking for from their coaches. The number one factor was the effectiveness of the coaching process, followed by personal compatibility, personal rapport, the coach's confidence and coach-specific training. So in other words, executives are looking for two crucially important factors:

1. Does this coach get results?
2. Can I work with him or her?

Those are the primary issues your marketing and all of your communications need to reflect - your results and your ability to build and maintain rapport. Your credentials as a coach are usually not the primary decision-making point for executives. Credentials are a benefit, but they won't determine whether you're hired.

There's a series of secondary factors too, including your personal gravitas and ability to relate to the executive as a peer, your level of coach-specific training, your sense of humor, how well you communicate your process, your reputation, and how experienced you are as a coach.

Ian: The final factor from the study is what methods and information the executive relies on when selecting a coach. The most commonly used and influential source is personal referrals or word of mouth. Thirty-eight percent of respondents said that was their most influential information source compared to 8 percent who said they knew the coach before and 8 percent who attended a seminar run by the coach. Only 6 percent made their choice primarily based on the coach's website.

Now, of course, there's a general trend across all buying decisions that more and more purchases are being made based on websites and other online factors, and we're sure that will continue. However, because of the very personal nature of coaching and because it has such a significant impact on the individual and organization its highly likely that referrals and personal recommendations will remain the most influential sources for some time to come.

In summary, executive clients are looking for support across a broad range of issues from a coach who delivers results and is easy to work with effectively. And the primary way they find that coach is by personal referrals backed up by a solid website and any live events where they've seen you.

Suzi: While that's what buyers of executive coaching are looking for in general, every specific client is different. What one client seeks as evidence of the results they're looking for, another one may not. And what one client is looking for in a coaching relationship, another one might not. When you're face-to-face with a specific client, you can work on figuring out that individual's specific needs - those things that are unique to that executive that are going to get him or her to say yes to you.

Your Perspective - What Kind of Client Are You Looking For?

All of us tend to work better and prefer to work with certain types of clients rather than others. Whether it is gender or age or a certain sector or executives with a specific challenge like communications or self-confidence, there is a group that we click with or resonate with best. When you're setting out to find clients to work with, you should focus on finding *your* ideal clients. Not every client you work with will be perfect for you, especially early on, but the clearer the picture you have of your ideal client, the more likely you are to find them and the more likely you are to end up working with them.

To a certain degree, this gets into the area of focusing on a niche. But for now, no matter what niche you're in or whether you have a specific niche, you'll absolutely have a type of client that's ideal to you. It's less important that you establish an industry niche or a niche in some specific subject matter expertise when you're first starting out and building your client base. But it is really important that you have a type of client so that *you* know who you work best with and for whom you can produce the most results.

In order to find or attract that type of client, you need to go through a process of figuring out some more details about what they look like and how you'll know if you're finding the right ones. What are their specific challenges, what are their specific aspirations, and what are they looking for in a coach? If you really nail these, you'll be able to communicate with them in ways that feel like you're speaking directly to them and give the impression that you really get them; you understand their reality and their world.

Ian: There are many ways of building understanding of your ideal clients. In this section we're going to show you a simple but comprehensive method you can use for your own clients. If you have your own preferred method, that's fine. The key is to find a method that works for you and use it.

An ideal client persona is an in-depth analysis of the key characteristics, demographics, interests, goals and aspirations, problems and issues of a typical target client for you. Rather than taking an average or summary across all your client types, you dive into details for one, two, or up to three of the most typical ones. By doing that, you can pull out the specifics that create real insight into what will motivate that type of client to buy from or hire you.

You're going to start by reviewing your experience and thinking through some of the best clients you've worked with - the sort you'd love to have again or have more of, that you really enjoy working with, or for whom you've gotten the best results. Or if you're relatively new, think about the sort of person you'd like to coach: What really gets you excited?

And then we're going to draw up what the marketing folks call a persona or avatar - but really it's just a way of making this idea of your ideal client more concrete so you can draw real and tailored insights from it rather than just broad generalizations.

Take a look at the Ideal Client Profile Map at the end of this chapter, or refer to it at the Library of Professional Coaching (where you can download one to work with). http://libraryofprofessionalcoaching.com/marketing/executive-coach-marketing-resource-centre/

You're going to start by reviewing your experience and thinking through some of the best clients you've worked with.

If you're a new coach without any previous clients, you'll have to extrapolate, of course. Later on we'll show you how to use informational interviews to build up an understanding of your potential clients. For now, think about the sort of person you'd like to coach - what really gets you excited.

Your avatar is a simplified picture of the common factors your ideal clients share. You'll draw it up for an individual as a way of making your ideal client more concrete for you so you can gain specific insights from it rather than just broad generalizations.

A quick caveat here: If you work with a diverse range of people it can be quite tough going to do this, but it will really help and it's worth persevering to get it done. If necessary, you can draw two or three different personas to represent different types of ideal clients but let's just start with one.

We're going to cover four areas with this persona. Start by writing down who this person is and their core demographics. Give them a name and write down if they're married, what age they're likely to be, and their gender. If you have a real balance of both men and women, just pick one for the sake of your persona. Note whether they have kids along with any other factors that will help you build a clear mental image. If you have a previous client who exactly fits the bill - someone you want to clone and get more of - then you can just base it around that profile, or an amalgam of several actual people.

Then get down to education. Are they college educated, or have some specialist education? Maybe they've worked their way from the shop floor? Write their back-story: How did they get to that executive role? Have they made frequent moves from company to company? Have they stayed in one function or moved between different functions? That can make a huge difference to the sort of issues they face in their role. Do they actually own the business or own part of it? Do they report to a more senior executive or does the buck stop with them? The challenges of executives in family-owned businesses, for example, even very large ones, are very often different from those of executives in shareholder-owned businesses.

Then think about some of the more psychological factors that make them tick. Why did they get into this business in the first place? What excites them? Which part of their role do they typically relish? Who do they admire: Is it CEOs of big businesses, fast-moving entrepreneurs, people who do things a bit differently or who play by the rules, sports heroes, or business people? Of course, you're not necessarily going to be able to characterize all of these factors for your ideal client, but the more you can, the more concrete you can make the persona, the more useful it's going to be.

Next, consider external pressures. Here you're going to write down the typical goals and targets that are set for your ideal client externally. Do they have tough growth or profit targets set? Is their industry all about cost cutting? Is this sort of business under threat from new competitors or new technology? Is it the sort of business that's under external regulation and scrutiny, as the nuclear and pharmaceutical sectors often are? Do they have a demanding CEO or chairman they report to? Again, depending on your ideal client, you may have a lot here or you may not have quite so much, but write down as much as you can.

Then, think about internal goals and aspirations. In other words, the things that the executives themselves are looking to achieve. Is your ideal client someone looking to leave a legacy then retire? Or are they younger executives looking to make a big splash and then maybe move on to a bigger role? Think about their big goals and ambitions. Then think small: Look at their typical day-to-day problems and issues, the things they often grumble about, the things that often get in the way of them achieving what they want.

Finally, move to the "know and feel" section. This is where you look at all the factors you've identified so far about your ideal client and then write down what would they need to "know and feel" to be ready to hire you. You need to capture both rational and emotional factors here - thus, know *and* feel. It could be that your ideal client has ambitious growth goals for their business and they work in a very competitive sector, so they need to know that you've helped executives succeed under those same pressures. Or they may have the self-confidence issues we saw reported in the survey and they want to feel that you'll empathize with them, that you'll be patient but you'll be persistent and get results.

It's often a good idea to think about the typical reasons why clients may not hire you or the objections they might have - the risks they might see in working with you. You might be an otherwise perfect match, but people worry about losing face in public by being seen to need a coach, for example or they might not sure you'll be able to stick with them for the long term. Sometimes these perceived risks can derail the buying process so you need to understand them and address them.

Mapping out your ideal client profile will help set the stage for finding and attracting those clients. It means you'll know whom to look for, and if you're asking for referrals, you can tell people exactly who would be a great client for you. This exercise can also help you put the right things on your website that will make your ideal clients feel like you understand them and deal with the issues they need resolved. Best of all, when you talk with them, you'll build that compatibility and rapport quickly, which is critically important to executives when they're looking to hire a coach.

Suzi: Executive coaches looking to do ideal client mapping often think to start with the organizations that they want to get into. You'll notice that Ian did not mention to make a list of every corporation you want to work in. If you've been thinking about or planning from that direction, try this approach instead. The approach that Ian has been describing will help you pinpoint the *individual* you're looking to target and not a corporate brand or faceless organizational entity. Remember that two-thirds of the time, the individual drives the decision to hire a coach.

The Question of Inexperience

Suzi: Newer coaches often ask us, "What if I don't have a lot of experience?" The answer is that you *do* need experience. When you are coaching senior executives, you've got to be able to position yourself and work with them at a peer level, otherwise they just won't hire you. It's about having and demonstrating gravitas or confidence and your ability to speak their language. While asking great questions and having mastery of a solid coaching process means that you should be able to help them if you do get hired, most executives are looking for more than that. They are looking for someone who understands and has experience in their world, with their challenges and situation. They want results.

Without that experience or gravitas, then it's a bit like trying to coach in a foreign language; you can speak on the basic level but you can't catch subtle nuances of what people are saying, or what they are not saying but others who speak that language know they meant. You can get away with it, but it's going to be painful and slow for you and for the executive, as they'll have to explain words and concepts that are not familiar to you. In that case, they're not going to get as much from working with you as they would from working with someone who has operated at the leadership or board level before and speaks fluent leadership.

Senior leaders respect someone who can stand up to them when needed or call their bluff, which you will be able to do effectively because of your own experiences. That means if you've got limited experience, you're unlikely to get hired by the more senior executives no matter how great your marketing is. The chemistry just won't work. But it doesn't mean that the experience you already have isn't relevant and useful in your business development process, or for less senior executives and leaders.

Ian: If you're in the position where you have some experience but not that senior level experience, I recommend focusing on something very specific and functional that executives would value even if you don't have a lot of senior level experience. If you specialize in coaching executives on time management, for example, that's not something where they would necessarily feel the need for you to have decades of executive experience. You're coaching them on something very specific and technical, so they would base a decision on your expertise in that area rather than your experience at an executive level. You don't need to have dealt with tricky people issues or other matters at an executive level for them to appreciate that you really know how to do time management. Over time, once you've earned more credibility as well as their respect, then they will often open up and begin to work with you on wider level things.

Pro-Bono Work

Suzi: It sounds like a catch-22, but if you don't have much experience and you want to coach at the executive level, you have to find a way to get that experience. That could mean working pro-bono for the board of a nonprofit, or it could mean paying your dues and working your way up by coaching at more junior levels first and then moving upwards with the same people or in the same organization once you have contextual understanding or a proven track record of results. The more you understand your ideal clients and what they need, the more you're going to come across as being in tune with them and able to lead them. But at the end of the day, there's no real shortcut to experience.

Please note: There is an important difference between actual pro-bono work and giving away free coaching sessions as part of your business development strategy (which we never recommend). Many coach training programs and schools teach their students that you should offer free sessions to give people a "taste" of what coaching can do for them. The truth of the matter is, however, that it's much harder to convert a free customer into a paying customer. Imagine you have a favorite coffee shop that you've been going to once a week for years, and you park in the same parking lot every time you go. Then one day you show up and they've put a meter in your parking lot. You now have to pay to park at the same place you've been parking for years for free. Obviously you're going to have a reaction to that, and you're probably going to park further away and walk just to avoid having to pay for the parking that you've been receiving for free.

One of the arguments you might hear in favor of offering something for free is that if you go into an ice cream shop, they'll give you a little spoonful to taste the ice cream before you make a purchase. But coaching and ice cream could not be more different. If an ice cream shop gives away a tiny spoonful of a two- or three-dollar cup of ice cream, can a little taste cost them more than five cents? When you are a coach, your product is hours of your coaching time. But you only have twenty-four hours in a given day, and no one allots all twenty-four of those to coaching services. Let's say, realistically, you have somewhere between six and ten billable hours in a given day. If you make even one of those available to a client for free, then you're giving away anywhere from a sixth to a tenth of your product. There is no company on the planet that is going to stay in business giving out that much free product. That's why it's not a useful metaphor.

Ian: The other thing about the ice cream analogy is that you can tell from one small bite of ice cream what the rest will taste like. With coaching, the first thirty minutes of coaching is set up. It doesn't adequately represent the whole, and so the free sample is not a proper one.

Suzi: Let's look at the issue differently, however. Pro-bono coaching work is a huge service to the community and to the planet and to organizations and to individuals, and I do recommend it in the context of charity work, or as we mentioned previously to bolster your own personal experience working with executives. But make sure that you are very protective of your pro-bono coaching time and that you are delivering pro-bono coaching services as an act of service, not as a marketing strategy. Give these services to those who otherwise couldn't afford to pay for it or to those you truly believe in and are passionate about the cause. Do it as an in-kind charity donation, a gift, for all the great reasons that people contribute to charities. Pro-bono work is great for giving back to your community or to build your track record, but it should not be done as a means to get a client.

What you *can* give away for free is a strategy session or consultation, because essentially that is a sales meeting. You're not pretending it's a full coaching session because that would be a little bit dishonest. You can accomplish some movement in one coaching conversation, but if typically you sell a six-month or full-year coaching engagement, one session is not going to show them what they're going to get for six months to a year with you. That's why it is a little bit incongruent to say I'll give you a free coaching session and then you'll have to decide whether you want to do this or not. You're better off giving them a free strategy session or consultation about their needs, which will help you both come to an understanding about whether moving forward is the right thing to do.

Ian: Some of the coach training that's available that advocates giving away a free coaching session is rather misleading. When you take the training, you discover that what they call a free coaching session is really just a sales meeting in which you talk with the client about where they are now, where they want to be, and the barriers in between, and then plot out a path for getting there. That's valuable for clients, but it's not coaching, it's a consultation and should not be confused with pro-bono work.

To Niche or Not to Niche

Ian: One of the other questions that gets asked a lot is, "Should I focus on a niche for my coaching practice?" I think we're going to differ here from a lot of advice you may have heard before.

Normally the advice you get is that you absolutely have to have an ultra-specific niche or you couldn't possibly succeed at all. That's patently not true. There are plenty of executive coaches making a good living without a very tight niche; some even do brilliantly well with it. Having a niche can certainly help with marketing by giving you focus and making it easier for you to get a clear picture of your ideal client so you can speak their language. Specializing can also create the perception that you really understand the issues and you're in tune with clients in that niche. Of course the more you work in that niche, the more true that perception becomes. If you look at the exercise we did to develop an ideal client profile, that's something that becomes very focused if you do work in a tight niche.

But it's not mandatory. And in particular, you really shouldn't let the question of which niche you could be in paralyze you. Don't go round and round with it and avoid doing any marketing because you haven't settled on your niche yet. Either pick one to go with temporarily as a test or just be a generalist and get your other marketing machines working harder for you.

Suzi: An important point here is that sometimes your niche finds you. I had a couple of clients in a corporate law department, and that went well and because they saw value, they referred me to the people that they knew, which happened to be in the legal sector too. Although I'm not a lawyer, I ended up coaching attorneys, corporate law department leaders, judges, and others - and it worked out well because it was a good fit with my skills and capabilities, but it wasn't anything I set out to do deliberately. As I got more and more lawyer clients, I began to build a reputation in that sector and it became self-perpetuating. But I never set out to niche myself in the legal market. Another example of a niche finding me is that a few years later, I did some work with a PhD scientist and started to get referrals to other PhD scientists. This goes back to what Ian was saying before about having multiple personas defined. I can define the persona of the corporate lawyers or the corporate legal executives or law firm leaders, but I can also define the persona of PhD scientists working in an arena where they need grant money and funding from the federal government. So I have two distinct personas to define, neither of which I intended as a niche but they unfolded based on who I was serving and the results that they were able to achieve. Sometimes your niche finds you and you want to be open to that possibility as well.

Ian: The critical thing is not to let yourself get paralyzed. I see many coaches who are doing almost no marketing at all because they haven't found their niche. That's counter-productive. If you do find a niche that works well for you, that's brilliant. But if you don't, just get on with it and do good marketing and good work, and you can either continue working generally or you'll find a niche that works for you at some point.

Be Prepared to Lead

Suzi: Coaches often ask us, "What if your potential clients don't actually know what they are looking for?" It's not uncommon. Executives frequently do not know what they want or need. In fact, they often might think they need team building and really they need to understand how to motivate their employees. That, of course, is not team building at all; it's the executive communication skill that needs strengthening.

This exposes two issues: The first is that you have to be prepared to lead them. You've got more experience in executive coaching than they have, so you know what executives typically get from working with you and the sort of challenges that they bring to coaching. You can suggest to them some of the value that other clients have received from your coaching to help the person in front of you crystalize his or her own needs.

Ian: The second issue is that from a marketing perspective, you have to focus on the symptoms that they actually do know about. They don't necessarily know what they want in terms of coaching but they do know about their problems, challenges, aspirations, and goals. Most executives don't necessarily think they need coaching, but they do know they have problems to solve and goals to reach. That's what you're going to focus your marketing on, not on coaching itself.

In the next chapter, we're going to talk about some of your options for how you will go about finding those ideal clients!

Toolbox

Know Your Client - Decision Makers at the Organizational Level

As you know from your own experience selling coaching services to complex systems, there are three, sometimes four, types of person involved in hiring an executive coach in an organization.

Usually the decision is primarily up to the executive, the client you'll be working with. Sometimes a more senior executive will "appoint" a coach for some of their team.

And sometimes - for instance when an organization is buying a program of coaching for a group of people rather than hiring a coach for a specific person - the vice president of human resources or someone similar will take the lead.

Even when the decision is made by the executive, it will not be in a vacuum. Chances are that the executive may check with the CEO, or there may be corporate rules about certification or pre-approved vendors.

And, of course, in most corporate organizations, any major purchases and sometimes some quite small ones have to run through an official procurement process, and the procurement officer or head of that department may need to be involved.

Even if you deal primarily with the situation in which the executive is the sole decision maker, it's still wise to understand what those other stakeholders are looking for.

Use the chart below to map your knowledge of the decision makers who buy executive coaching services and discover what you need to learn about each one to best customize your approach and offer to suit their needs and interests.

Company	Decision Maker Name & Title	Goals & Aspirations	Challenges	Key Factors in Decision	Who He or She Influences	Who He or She is Influenced by

Ideal Client Profile Map

Know Your Client - Individual Executive Level: Ideal Client Profile Mapping

You may eventually have up to three personas that represent three ideal clients, but we have to start with the first. Think about the following:

1. What are some defining characteristics and common factors that make clients like that a great fit?

Reality Check:

2. Are there enough of those types of clients to make the economics work for you?

3. Can they afford to pay for your services?

4. Are they used to paying for this sort of service?

5. Can you reach them with your marketing?

Data gathering: Once you've decided on one ideal client persona, gather all the information you have on that type of client. Start by documenting what you already know about them. If possible, narrow it down to a specific individual to keep in mind during this process.

6. Make a list of everything you know about this client.

7. Do you have any market research data to incorporate into your analysis?

8. Do you have gaps in your knowledge? If yes, what market research do you need to do?

9. Do you want to survey or ask clients or potential clients in order to discover their big problems and challenges as well as their goals and aspirations?

10. If so, who will you survey or ask?

Creating Your Ideal Client Profile

Drawing out and organizing the information you have about your clients in the following form allows you to extract actionable insights that you can use in your marketing efforts going forward. The chart below starts with obvious, surface-level observations and then goes deeper into factors that drive the ideal client's behavior.

First, it helps to start with an actual photo or drawing of a real person who fits your ideal client profile, as it makes it more real and will help you to produce a more detailed and useful persona.

Then divide your paper into these four quadrants, or use four separate pages to record your thinking about and responses to the guiding questions in each box on the Ideal Client Profile Map.

Ideal Client Profile Map with guiding questions:

A. Who They Are	B. Their External Targets and Pressures
Summarize all the basic facts, figures, and demographics your know about this ideal client: Age? Gender? Married? Kids? Education level? Work experience? Career path? Current role? Interests outside of work? Who do they admire? Who do they hate? Religion? Politics? What's their backstory of how they got to where they are today?	Identify the key external drivers that drive the behavior of your ideal client: If they run a business, what profit and growth targets? What moves are competitors making? How are their customers changing? New legislation? Environmental issues? Changes in their supplier base? If employed, what targets have been set by their boss? What are shareholders expecting? What is the board expecting? What media influences do they face? What is impacting their career? What pressures are they under?
C. Their Internal Aspirations and Challenges	**D. "Know and Feel" Factors**
Write down everything you know about your ideal client's internal landscape: What are their personal goals? What are their career and life aspirations? What are their current challenges? Are there any big challenges they face every day? What's keeping them up at night? What day to day annoyances do they face? What stands in their way? What do they complain about? What do they worry about?	What would your ideal clients need to know and feel to be comfortable hiring you: Do they need to know you've worked with people like them? Do they need to know about the great results you've achieved with your clients? Do they need to now you're an expert in their industry or functional area? Do they need to feel they could work with you personally? Do they need to know they're similar to other clients who've achieved the sort of results they're looking for? Do they need to know you'd push them when they need it or empathize and be sensitive to their situation? What are the objections they might have to hiring you?

Checklist for Action: Networking Ideas

Use this action checklist to kick start your networking activities if you don't know where to start or if you just want to get your networking unstuck.

1. List the categories in your life in which you know people (i.e., family, church, work, neighborhood, school, past employers, business associates, friends, associations or professional groups, and those who provide services to you (such as your dentist, etc.).
2. Make each category a separate page and list all the people you know in each category, or use the Relationship Asset Inventory.
3. In each category, choose the top three people you know best and feel most comfortable reaching out to as your networking starters.
4. Set up time to talk to or be with your network starters, seek to learn about what matters most to them, and tell them your vision.
5. Ask your network starters who else they know that you could talk to about your vision.
6. Seek out every person your network starters referred you to, seek to learn about what matters most to them, and tell them your vision.
7. Ask each of these people who else they know that you might talk to.
8. Continue to work your way through your own network lists.
9. Continue to follow up and meet people from your network starters' networks.
10. Tell everyone you meet what you are up to in your business and be curious about what they are up to in their business, career, life.
11. Explore partnering and alliance-building opportunities.
12. Share a clear profile of your ideal clients, plant seeds for referrals, and ask for introductions.
13. You can ask for introductions in this way, referencing your ideal client and what you do to help solve a challenge common to your ideal clients: "Do you happen to know anybody who is X, needs Y, or could use Z?" For instance, "Do you happen to know anyone who is a C-level female leader of an organization who needs to find innovative ways to influence or could use help finding her unique leadership point of view?"
14. Another way to ask is, "Do you or anyone you know ever find that you have N challenge?" For instance, "Do you or anyone you know ever find that you

have a hard time motivating your employees, or improving their engagement at work?"

15. Identify and list at least ten people with whom you want to do a collaborative joint venture and explore possibilities with them.

16. Make a list of everyone you know who is in an industry or organization that aligns with those you most like to coach, or where you get the best results.

CHAPTER 3

The Marketing Mindset

Suzi: Cultivating and sustaining a marketing mindset is a key ingredient in the Coach Approach to Finding New Clients. Whether you're new coach or a seasoned veteran, you already know that in order to make the difference you want to make in the world through your executive clients in the corporations and organizations that you serve, you've got to create opportunities to coach. Mindsets are critical to your business development success. You could take all the right actions, but if your mindsets are incongruent, then your results will be subpar. When you're focused on coaching clients, you know the importance of having the right mindsets, and you should use that understanding to your advantage because it holds true in your business development as a coach.

Ian: In this chapter we're going to run through a number of mindsets or factors that we've found to be helpful when it comes to finding and winning clients. We're not saying that you have to switch everything you do and think exactly like we do about marketing, but take a look at some of these mindsets. Take a look at some of your own thought patterns about marketing and evaluate whether those thoughts and mindsets might actually be holding you back.

Action Orientation Mindset

Ian: The first mindset we like to talk about is what we call having an action orientation. Coaches typically have quite a passive mindset to marketing. They think, "If I do good work, people will hear about me, and people will want to come and do business with me." Sometimes you hear that passive mindset expressed as "Word of mouth is the best marketing."

Now, of course, word of mouth is certainly an excellent form of marketing. But if the only marketing you're doing is relying on other people speaking about you to potential new clients, then you're going to be in trouble.

Another sign of a passive mindset is when you hear people say, "something will turn up" or "once the recovery kicks in, I'll be okay." That kind of passive mindset - just hoping something will happen - is not going to be effective. Obviously we'd advise you to take a more action-oriented view of marketing, to choose to take action rather than just hoping something is going to happen.

Suzi: Hope is not a business development strategy. Magic is not a business development strategy. Word of mouth does make business a lot easier to develop, but it doesn't preclude you or excuse you from being the master of your actions and making sure that you're taking action to get the results that you want

Partnership Mindset

Ian: The second mindset we'd like to talk about is having a partnership mindset to marketing. There are really two components to that. One is having a client service mindset. Realizing that it's not about pushing your stuff on clients irrespective of whether they want it or not. It's about helping them and doing your best for them.

But this needs to be combined with having confidence and valuing your own capabilities. Your approach to clients shouldn't be about being subservient, or about being happy if someone throws you scraps from the table. It should be about understanding that there are two beneficiaries in a partnership: you benefit because they pay you, but they benefit just as much from the great coaching and the great results they receive as result of working with you.

If you don't have that partnership mentality, I believe it's difficult to be a good coach. If you always see yourself as subservient to your client, there are certain things you can't do with them as their coach.

Suzi: I can tell a little story that illustrates the power of the mindset of being in service, and why that mindset being primary makes a huge difference in the results that you can produce in your marketing and business development actions. When I first started my coaching business (we're going back twenty-two years now), I had some screwy mindsets about what sales meant or about what marketing meant or about what business development meant. In my mindset, it was akin to the intrusive persona of the stereotypical used car salesman - someone who was pushy or forcing themselves on you - and I didn't want to be that. I didn't want to be aggressive and manipulative. As a result of that mindset, after my first year and a half in business, I was $10K in debt and living off of credit cards. What made all the difference for me was this particular mindset shift that we're talking about now. Once I shifted my mindset to one of client service, helping people, making a difference, and seeking to contribute, I was debt-free and earning a sustainable, six-figure income within six months.

Ian: That's what mindset can do: everything else follows. You won't do all the great marketing activities we're going to teach you if you haven't got the mindset right. Or you'll try to do them, but you won't do them well.

Suzi: That's right. You can take all the right actions, but if your mindset is not congruent with your passions, intentions, service to your clients, and service to the relationships that you're building, then your results are not going to be what you want them to be.

Ian: I have noticed an almost schizophrenic or "flip-flop" mentality among executive coaches because, just as you had Suzi, a lot of people who become executive coaches often come from an executive background themselves or from a helping or service background, and they have this impression that marketing equals used car sales person.

Nobody wants to be that kind of pushy person so they almost go to the extreme in other direction. They don't do any marketing at all. That, of course, holds them back and almost prevents them from doing anything. But then they suddenly become desperate because they have no clients coming in so they flip-flop in the other direction and become the terrible pushy person that they didn't want to be out of desperation.

But of course, there's a big middle ground in between doing nothing and being pushy and aggressive. You can absolutely do great marketing that brings on clients without it feeling pushy to them or to you. In fact, in many ways, given the great gifts that you have, what you can do, and the results your clients achieve by working with you, in many ways you're doing them a disservice if you don't make them aware of what you can do. If they would benefit from working with you, then you're letting them down by not giving them that opportunity.

Suzi: You have to do it in a way that is aligned with your natural style and personality. One of the things that we want to challenge you to think about is any mindsets you hold that are causing you to get in your own way. By taking time to identify any assumptions or sets of beliefs that might be holding you back, you can see what you might need to shift in order to get the results you're looking for. You don't have to stop and do this right now, but it is something to spend time thinking about.

Always-Be-Networking Mindset

Ian: The always-be-networking mindset is about making sure that you are building your contact network at every available opportunity.

Networking is much more than just formal networking events, breakfast meetings, evening mixers, and so forth. Networking is about connecting with people - being human. It happens in non-work situations when you're working on school committees or attending social events or even when you're just waiting in a line somewhere and you have the opportunity to talk to the person next to you and establish a connection there. It can even happen when you're being served yourself - getting your hair cut or having someone repair the plumbing in your house.

Even those people who you think don't have connections to executives are important to connect with. You just never know what it might come to, and it costs you nothing to do that. You can either just ignore people or you can be social and network.

Suzi: I want to underscore the point about never knowing what connections might exist where you don't expect them. The plumber who comes to your house might have a sister or cousin or uncle who's an executive or married to an executive. You just never know.

Ian: You wouldn't deliberately call lots and lots of plumbers to your house in order to talk to them because the probability of making a connection to your target client is low, but since the plumber is already there in your house, it costs you nothing and it takes no extra time to just talk to them and ask them about their business. Eventually the conversation will come around to your business.

I'm sure you've heard yourself hundreds of stories of accidental meetings in airports, check-out queues, and coffee shops that ultimately led to fruitful coaching relationships or referrals for someone, or, at a minimum, just a more pleasant day.

Suzi: It's an important point you're raising, Ian, because we're so busy generally, and I noticed here in the United States, it seems like time is speeding up and people are busier than ever before. So a lot of times when we talk to people about "always be networking," they say, "Well, I don't have time for networking. I don't have time to go to extra things or to go out of my way to create networking conversations." The point that you raised with the plumber example is a good one, which is that you don't have to go out of your way to add more things into an already busy schedule. Just take advantage of the people you run into all day long, every day. As you're out and about doing the things that are meaningful to you - whether you're picking up children from school, participating in community activities, or attending religious services, do what you're already doing but with a conscious mindset of networking. That way, you will take advantage of those unplanned or accidental opportunities to strike up a conversation with the people around you; whereas if you don't have a mindset of "always networking," you wouldn't necessarily take up that opportunity. It doesn't take extra time to seek the opportunities that exist around you.

Ian: This willingness to always be networking is the real differentiator because very few people actually do it. It's much easier to stand in that queue in silence or work at a community event and just do the job, than it is to take the extra effort to connect with people and find out more about them, what they do, and what's important to them. It's just easier when you're busy to do the minimum, but in reality it only takes a little extra effort to actually connect with people - and, as we've said, something may just come from it.

Suzi: You've got to bring a genuine curiosity. If you didn't have that curiosity, you wouldn't be seeking out those conversations or exploring them. You also have to continuously have a focus on other people and not on yourself. When I get on an airplane, I am often tired and just want to sleep, but then when I realize that's me focusing on myself, I can snap out of it. I realize that if I focus on the people around me, I will have a new level of engagement. Fortunately, the natural curiosity that we bring as coaches works for us powerfully in the networking aspect of finding prospective clients.

Ian: Overcoming tiredness is a big deal. I was just talking to someone last night at an event for professional speakers and we had just gone there to learn something. But as she was saying, she really had to make a choice about going out versus staying home, cuddling up under a blanket, and watching TV. She chose to go out and meet people. She didn't really know what it would lead to, but by talking to attendees between the sessions and listening to their stories, she made half a dozen really useful connections. That wouldn't have happened had she chose either to stay at home and watch TV or to just go along and listen to the presentation but not interact or get involved. That focus on others versus what you want leads us to the mindset of "understanding the game."

Understanding-the-Game Mindset

There are many elements to the game of marketing. The first thing is you've got to know your clients. You've got to understand their goals, aspirations, problems, and challenges. You also have to understand what they value and admire. You've got to have the mindset of being curious and interested in your clients and caring about them.

You also have to have the mindset of understanding your process. What are the different stages to bringing a client on board? What do you do to first to connect with them? What's the next step? What comes after that? What happens just before you bring them on as a client? You have to understand your process step-by-step rather than seeing it as a random series of unconnected events in which you make up what to do next on the spot. By understanding these stages, you always know what to do next.

Suzi: That's important because you need to lead the process. Maintaining this mindset of understanding your process plus leadership during the conversation is critical in the business development, networking, marketing, and sales process. You want to not only know your process but lead the potential client through your process. Don't assume that they're in charge of the process because then you'll end up back to the strategy of hope, which, as we know, is not a good business development strategy. This can be challenging for us as coaches, because it is different from our coaching engagements. In a coaching engagement, the client is often the leader and we're following their agenda.

Ian: There's an interesting balance you have to draw because nobody wants to feel as if they are being pushed and manipulated and maneuvered. But at the same time potential clients are very willing to give up control because they don't know what the right steps are to figure out whether they should be working with you. You've done that many more times than they have. As long as they know you're going to be open with them and not manipulate them, then they're happy to let you lead.

Suzi: This is especially effective if you're being of service in addition to coming from a mindset of service. You're starting to see how all of these mindsets integrate. If you're coming truly from a mindset of service, focused on what's best for your client, and you've built that rapport and trust, then they're going to be more than willing to be gently guided through the process. The reason I'm emphasizing the importance of leading is because this is the place where I often see coaches abdicate control and do whatever the client wants, deluding themselves that it's in the context of being of service. But truly, the client doesn't always know what they want. They come to you because they think they want one thing, but in seeking to know and understand your clients and understand your clients, you might discover that what they really need is something that's the precursor to what they're asking for. So there are opportunities for you to gently guide and lead, and it's an opportunity for you to serve the client.

Ian: Doing what's best for the client isn't necessarily what they happen to want at a given time or think they want. Part of your role is to understand the bigger picture and help your client discover it.

Ian: The final aspect of understand the game is that you have to understand the numbers. As you go through your process for bringing clients on board, you need to be very aware of questions like these: How many initial contacts do you need to get a first meeting with a client? How many meetings are actually needed? How long does it take? How much follow up do you need in between? How many meetings do you need before one of them will turn into a client? Of course, these are rules of thumb rather than exact numbers that come out the same every time. But you need to know these numbers because they tell you day in and day out whether you are making enough initial contacts.

Because the overall process for bringing a client on board is usually quite long, you need to keep your eye on this. You can't just measure progress based on the number of new clients you've got right now; you've got to know what it's going to look like in the future. You've got to know whether you're bringing enough people into your pipeline, into your field of influence, so that downstream you'll be bringing enough clients on board.

Suzi: You also have to know your timeline, which goes back to knowing your process, but it's tied in with knowing your numbers. It's useful to know how long it takes you. Your timeline will vary based on your target market, the niche that you're working in, and your credibility, expertise, and experience in that community or industry. Some people may take many months or a year to close a client, and for some people it may be one rather quick conversation. Part of understanding your own timeline is knowing what to expect and how to manage everything around that - your activities, the calls that you're making, the number of people that you're meeting, how you structure your finances, and so forth. It's important to know your personal system and process and timeline so you can manage them.

Ian: Your timeline will also vary depending on the mode of marketing. If you get a referral from someone very close to your potential client and that person who referred you knows that the person is looking for an executive coach right now, then the chances are that's going to be a fairly short process. But if we return to the plumber example and the plumber introduces you to his brother who works for an organization but he isn't the executive who might need your support, then there could be many, many steps and it could take much, much longer. You have to understand that the type of marketing dramatically influences the timeline.

The Persistence Mindset

Ian: When it comes to bringing on clients, there really is no silver bullet. There's not one specific action you can pick from this book that you can quickly put in place to change everything overnight. Change will more likely come from implementing lots of little things and getting them right regularly and consistently.

Related to persistence, it's worth remembering that you almost never win a client at first contact. It almost always takes consistent communication over time before they're ready. Marketing is not all about jumping from hot lead to hot lead. It's about consistently communicating, keeping in touch, and nurturing relationships with the people in your circle. Marketing is about building relationships and credibility so that when the time is right, you're the person that they call and ultimately end up working with.

Authenticity

Suzi: The undercurrent that runs through all of these mindsets is authenticity. For these mindsets to work for you, you have to love what you're doing and the community that you're seeking to create coaching opportunities within. If you're loving the organizations that you're coaching in, then that's going to show through to them and others loud and clear. The mindset is authentically aligning who you are and what you're doing with what matters most to you. You can do all the right things; you can be persistent, you can understand the game, you can always be networking, you can have a mindset of partnership and service and confidence in your capabilities, you can be action- oriented, but if you're not enjoying it, *truly* enjoying it, or if you're not engaged in the role and challenged by what you're doing, that's going to impact your ability to sign new clients. Likewise, if you're desperate for business, that's going to show through much louder than everything you're doing, too.

Check with yourself before you take action so that you can know that what you're doing is a true fit for you. If it's not, don't keep pushing forward in an area that's not a fit for you. Change directions. Pivot. Find another way to go. But keep checking in with yourself because if you're not getting the results that you want, chances are there is something out of whack in one of these mindsets. Shift your thoughts to shift your actions and results. Your mindset is the basis for everything.

Toolbox

Executive Coach Marketing Mindsets

We must each create opportunities to coach, and mindsets are critical to our business development success. Some beliefs, assumptions, and ways of thinking will help you market yourself effectively and win clients, and some of your thought patterns about marketing may be holding you back. Answering these questions will help you assess your mindsets and empower you to market yourself more effectively.

Action Orientation

What mindsets do I have that may be too passive?

What are my current mindsets about taking action to advance the results that I want in business development?

What are my fears related to marketing to executives?

If I find myself putting off contacting executives or taking action with my marketing – what are the thoughts going through my head What reasons am I giving myself for procrastinating?

Partnership Mindset

In what specific ways can I flip my mindset from one of sales to service?

List 3 – 5 great outcomes or results I've helped my clients to achieve.

List 3 – 5 skills or characteristics that I've had great feedback on from clients.

In what areas can I have more confidence in my capabilities and the results I help my clients to produce?

What mindsets or beliefs may be getting in my way or holding me back?

What mindset shifts do I want to make in order to improve my results?

Always Be Networking

What current opportunities do I have to connect with people that I've previously ignored as irrelevant? How can I reframe them and see them as networking opportunities?

Where am I already interacting with people that I could put extra effort into connecting with them and more fully explore possibilities?

What are three areas where I'm focused on myself that I could flip to focus on others?

Understand the Game

What do I need to know about my clients to really understand them?

What are the stages of my business development process?

Where am I ignoring the numbers? How could knowing those numbers allow me to take charge of my business results?

Do I update and review my business model and numbers based on real data from my recent marketing?

Persistence

In what ways can I reframe my current approach to plan for consistent, regular, and recurring actions?

What matters most to me with regard to my work as a coach?

How can I align the actions I'm consistently taking with what matters most

Mental Positioning Checklist: Critical Mindsets for Success

Use this checklist to align your mindsets for ultimate success in business development. Developing new business is not just about the actions you're taking. You can take all the right actions for growing your business but experience less than optimal results due to limiting beliefs or counterproductive mindsets.

1. Partnership
2. Be a connection seeker.
3. Sales is not a dirty word: Reframe sales as an extension of your service cycle – it is about helping your clients.
4. Approach sales from a service context: Use your coaching skills in a coach-approach to selling.
5. Ask, "How can I help?" Focus on service, taking care of others, being helpful
6. Do what you do - and think marketing.
7. Expect to grow your business by referrals. Give referrals and become refer-able. Referrals breed referrals.
8. Use social media, and embrace two degrees of separation.
9. Operate with integrity and business ethics.
10. Keep a broad view of who the client is (strive for depth in organizations).
11. Think long-term.
12. Develop and sustain long-term, meaningful relationships.
13. Use your natural and authentic sales style and approach: No tricks, gimmicks, or techniques will seal the deal for you.
14. Ask for specific help, referrals, leads, and business deals.
15. Listen more than you speak.
16. Provide exceptional service by making bold promises and overdelivering.
17. Learn what clients need, want, and expect, and then give them more.
18. Value is defined by the client, not by you.
19. Operate from a foundation of commitment, by articulating what you are committed to and finding out what is important to the client.
20. Act as if the potential client is already a client and treat them with that level of care through the sales process.
21. Follow through is critical.
22. Link individual goals with organizational goals and generate measurable results.
23. Every interaction is an opportunity for relationship.

24. Challenge assumptions: yours and theirs.
25. You are always in a sales conversation - either you're selling or you're being sold to.
26. You always have a choice.
27. Adopt an abundance mentality - believe you can make a difference AND make oodles of money.
28. Never give away free coaching samples! If you believe people need to have an experience of your service before buying, offer an introductory rate or a discounted sample rate rather than giving it away for free. If you give it away for free, you interfere with your own value proposition.

CHAPTER 4
The Marketing Menu: Coach Approach Options

I an: In this chapter we're going to look at the best ways to find and make initial contact with potential clients. Sometimes that initial contact is going to come from you reaching out directly to those potential clients and sometimes it's going to be more about putting yourself in a position for them to notice and reach out to you. It is really two ends of the marketing spectrum.

On one end you have marketing that involves you (or a common contact your potential client already trusts) interacting directly with a potential client in person. That could be meeting them face-to-face at an event, getting a referral, or doing a presentation they attend. This in-person marketing has more impact and takes you a long way down the road of bringing a client on board, because in person you've got the chance to interact and explore what they really need, demonstrate your capabilities, and give them a feel for what it would be like to work with you.

When you move to more impersonal hands-off marketing, you make less impact per person. If you send a letter or use an advertisement or they come to a website or see something you post on social media, you're not interacting personally so you can't build up much of a relationship. But you can reach more people with that marketing, often quite a lot more. These are good approaches for making initial contact with lots of potential clients that you can then work to interact with more directly later.

When it comes to marketing for executive coaches, we're going to talk primarily about what we call the coach approach, which is very much focused on the high-probability in-person approach because that's what's going to bring you the best results fast.

It is wise to add some other forms of marketing to that core approach, so in this chapter we will look at some less direct marketing methods that will get you into contact with more people and start your relationship with them. We also provide a "marketing menu" workbook at the end of this chapter. It's a more detailed guide to some of the most effective marketing approaches for executive coaches with guidelines on when each approach works best. We will be referring to two main factors with each of the marketing methods: *impact* and *reach*. In other words, how far does that method progress you down the path of bringing that potential client on board, and how many other potential clients will that method connect you with that could become potential clients later?

Suzi : There's no need to do everything on the menu of options all the time. We simply want to provide a menu of options so you can decide what resonates for you and your natural style. Seek to build a portfolio for yourself of maybe four or five different types of marketing methods, because you want to have multiple ways of reaching potential customers. Some of the methods are going to work better for you, and some of them are going to work better for your ideal clients, but you can create a balance. We don't want the menu to overwhelm you; on the contrary, we want you to feel free to choose so you don't become overwhelmed.

Ian: And every coach will have a different set of items on the menu that they'll use and maybe they'll try something new every now and then to see if that works, to see if they like it, to see if it gets results, but they'll have this core set of tools that they prefer to use.

Menu Option 1: Existing Client Development

The first approach on our menu is existing client development. The idea here is to expand your work with some of your current clients. This is often overlooked in favor of trying to bring in completely new clients. Of course a lot of your marketing is going to be about bringing in new clients, but don't overlook the business you can get from your existing clients.

For instance, if you're working with one executive or group of executives in a client organization, you can look to expand to other executives in that same part of the organization. Sometimes you're working with the chief executive and it's not appropriate to work with his or her team but it would be appropriate to work with other executives more laterally. Or it could be doing more work with the same executives by broadening the scope of what you're coaching them on, or coaching more frequently, or extending the length of your engagement. All, of course, provided that you're bringing them more value.

Another possibility is getting an internal referral to executives in other parts of the client's organization not directly related to the one you're working in. In this case you probably won't know those executives personally from the work you've been doing, but you can harness your good relationships to get introductions.

That type of marketing approach works for nearly all executive coaches as long as you have an existing client base. For anything other than small businesses, there are always other executives working in your clients' organizations, and because you should already have built up good levels of credibility and trust with your direct clients, they should be happy to make introductions for you. You may also already know some other executives because of your interactions as part of your work too.

Of course, if you're a start-up and don't have many clients at the moment, you'll have to look at other approaches.

This approach requires that you mentally step back from your work with your client and think creatively. What else can you offer? What else could be of value to your client and who else in the client organization could value what you do?

This also requires the courage to ask whether they could introduce you to another executive or would it be appropriate to be working with other executives in the organization to expand your reach.

Suzi: It's always an easier sale when you're within an organization, where you have a track record of proven results. They know you, and you also know them and can make the most of your time by forming more and better relationships.

I once spent some time coaching in the legal department of a multinational corporation. I was working with the vice president, and he and his team were located in offices in the same hallway, yet instead of getting up and talking to them, he communicated largely by email. He and his lieutenant could literally have just spoken through the wall, the walls were so thin, but they used email instead. Part of my work with him shifted his behavior to "walking the halls," building relationships, and being available. As I was doing walking the halls in the organization, not only did I meet more executives to work with, but I also met a woman who was always working there at the same time and appeared to be a consultant. Eventually she stopped me in the halls, introduced herself, and suggested we have a cup of coffee together. It was the beginning of a very lucrative connection for both of us. She was a consultant in an entirely different, yet complementary, arena to mine, so we were able to create a lot of additional business with each other because we were visible in the organization and were each seeking to develop more relationships within existing client relationships. There are always opportunities. The executive you are working with in an organization is not the only one. Be visible and make the most of your opportunities to generate and explore new possibilities to expand your client base within each client organization.

Ian: One simple idea is to arrange to meet with your client in a public area - either the canteen or in a meeting room - rather than their office. A common area gives you a chance to get out, and increases the likelihood your client will introduce you to other people in the organization that they know. Simple steps like that make a big difference. Being proactive about asking them if they can introduce you to people is also critical.

The impact of developing your existing clients is very high. For most executive coaches this should always be the first port of call if you're working in a corporate organization where there are other executives or other opportunities. Start there before you go further afield.

The reach of such efforts is obviously less than other approaches because you can only do that with your existing clients. It's not going to break open new organizations or provide huge numbers of new potential clients. However, for every one you do reach, you've got a very good chance for bringing them on as a client because you already have the internal stamp of approval within their organization.

Menu Option 2: Referrals

Suzi: There are opportunities with an existing client to break into new organizations in the form of referrals. The vice president of the multinational corporation I mentioned previously was on the board of directors for a nonprofit, and he connected me to the general counsel of a different corporation because she asked him at one of their board meetings about some executive coaching she needed and he referred me. So even though the reach is low, there's still an opportunity.

Ian: Referrals are really just an extension of the same principle. It's getting your existing clients, previous clients, and your contacts to recommend you to new people.

Again this is an approach that works for pretty much all executive coaches. Even if you're a start-up, the truth is you almost always already have a decent contact base. Maybe they're not people you've worked with as a coach, but people you worked with in an executive role, in previous jobs, or people you know socially. You always know some people who could introduce you to potential clients. Obviously it's going to be a stronger referral if they've worked with you, but personal connections help as well.

Suzi: There are four keys to referrals.

1. You must be giving excellent service. That's the baseline. If you're not doing an excellent job, don't expect to get referred no matter how often you ask.
2. You must continually plant seeds with your clients and express the importance of referrals to your business at the start and frequently throughout the engagement.
3. You must directly ask for referrals and be intentional about consistently requesting referrals and introductions. You can't just assume that by doing good work, clients will automatically refer you.
4. Always be considerate in acknowledging referrals either with a handwritten note or a gift or a sincere verbal acknowledgement, because that encourages people to continue to refer you and they feel appreciated for making referrals.

Ian: One thing that requires a little bit of work in advance that can really help with referrals is to make sure you have a clear and succinct definition of who exactly you're looking to be referred to. This helps the people you ask know who would be a good referral for you as well as the value you bring to the table to that person. That makes it much easier for them to spot opportunities to refer you and much more comfortable for them because they know how you can help.

That goes back to the idea of building a deep understanding of your ideal client. If you've done that and you can clearly communicate who those clients are and how you help that really helps people refer you to those people. That is much more effective than saying, "Can you refer me to anyone you know who might need my services?"

That is better than nothing but it won't help your clients figure out who to connect you with. Take the guesswork out of it for them.

The impact of referrals is high, because there is a transfer of trust. When the person who refers you is known and trusted by the person they're referring you to, then that makes it much easier for you to take them on board as a client.

The reach, again, is fairly low because each person you ask for referrals is only likely to have only one or at most a few to give you. But because the impact is so high, referrals are always where we start looking for new clients.

Menu Option 3: Networking Events

The next approach that many coaches try is networking events. We're distinguishing here between formal networking events and the idea we talked about previously: "always be networking." Networking events are formal organized events, including meet and greet mixes, breakfast networking events, lunch time networking events, chamber of commerce events, and so forth, in which the idea is that you meet potential clients and referrals face-to-face.

In order for formal networking events to be effective for you, you'll need a good return on your investment of time. Unlike the kind of networking we talked about earlier where you happen to be out and you use that as an opportunity to network without setting aside extra time, formal networking events require you to invest your discretionary time. Considering that, you need to go to events that are convenient for you and have a high percentage of target clients and referrers. When it comes to executive coaching, formal networking is a bit less effective than it might be for other types of coaches because it's relatively rare that senior executives go to normal networking events. In my experience in the UK, very senior executives and chief executives might go to private events like a Vistage event or the Academy of Chief Executives in the UK, which is similar. Or they might go to some industry- or sector-specific events, but the typical chamber of commerce or business networking events do not attract our target clients.

Suzi: It is the same in the States. Just keep in mind that not all networking events are created equal. When you're considering events, it is important to figure out who is coming to which events and what the purpose of each event is, and then discern whether is it a match for your objectives. For example, executives in organizations may be networking with other people at their same level at other organizations, or with their peers, or with their own target clients. They're more likely to be attending organized networking events if their organization and culture values a civic-minded approach and they are active on boards and local community events. In that case, you will find them, but they are typically not at networking events.

Ian: That's absolutely right. You have to figure out the right events. You may find that it's difficult for a coach to gain entry to some of these exclusive events where executives are networking with their peers unless you're very well established with people like them or in an industry sector. One way to get in is to be a speaker at the event. It's very senior people without suppliers or guests, and the best chance of a coach coming in is to be able to speak on a topic of interest to them.

Suzi: One issue to be aware of is that some of those C-suite organizations like Vistage and others may require you to pay to be a speaker, which I wouldn't recommend.

Ian: Now if you do find events that could work for you, then you have to have networking skills. You have to be genuinely interested in other people, have a "giving first" mentality, and be able to clearly articulate what you do when you're asked - who you help and how you help them. You also have to do your research to ensure you're going to the right events for you and for the senior executive decision-makers you wish to meet.

The typical impact of a networking event is relatively low. It's usually just an initial first contact. You're probably not going to meet a lot of executives at your typical networking event. If you hit the right networking event, of course, that could change, but generally the impact is low and the reach is medium.

Menu Option 4: Public Speaking

Ian: Giving talks or seminars allows you to showcase your capabilities and personality to your audience. If you can speak well and if you have a topic that's interesting and valuable to potential clients *and* you can find the right audience, then this can be an effective approach. If you're a really good speaker, you're more likely to get into an exclusive event than you are just as an attendee.

This approach obviously requires you to be an excellent speaker or seminar leader. If you're just a mediocre speaker, then this is probably not going to work for you. In addition, in order to get booked in events that senior executives are likely to attend, you need a strong reputation and a track record.

Suzi: I recommend not just taking any opportunity to speak. Make sure you'll be speaking to an audience filled with those who are in your sweet spot. It's also a good idea to make a very clear offer - a deal, a product, a coupon, or anything else that will compel them to come up and speak to you afterwards or to get them to follow up and contact you in the days and weeks to come. I've heard many stories from coaches who receive no sales benefit from giving a well-received talk. You want your specific offer to entice your potential clients to come to you based on your talk. Unlike referrals, which often lead to a meeting and discussion about potentially working together, public speaking usually provides an opportunity to begin a relationship with some follow up that then leads to a meeting later on.

Ian: Follow up is critical after public speaking opportunities because it's unlikely that someone is going to listen to you and then months later remember you if they find they need the services of an executive coach. So you want to make an offer in the talk that gets you talking to them one-to-one, and it could just be talking briefly after the event or for them to come and meet you one-to-one and have a discussion about how what you spoke about might be appropriate to their organization. The important thing is to have a way of transitioning from being on the stage talking to a group to talking to them one-on-one about potentially working with them. It's not enough to do a great talk and hope that people will remember you when they need you. You need some way of making that one-to-one connection with them. That specific offer is called a call-to-action.

Suzi: Managing your own expectations is also important. Don't expect to get a bunch of clients from one talk. It's rare that someone will come up to you after a talk and book you on the spot. It just doesn't usually work that way. So manage your expectations accordingly. Talks work better as a marketing tool, to raise awareness about your expertise and credibility, rather than as a direct sales vehicle.

In addition to having that opportunity to talk to them one-on-one, make sure you have a take-away or gift to give them that they won't throw away. You can also request their business card in exchange do a drawing to give away a book, CD, DVD, or something else of value that they might want. Or you can provide some low-cost gift that has your contact information on it. If you really need to go low budget, then at least make sure you have a handout that has something of tremendous value on it for them besides your contact information.

Ian: Ideally you want the opportunity to follow up with them proactively yourself. Asking for their business card in return for a chance to win a copy of a CD or a book allows you to send regular emails or other forms of follow-up.

If you get the follow-up sequence right, the impact can be quite high. The reach is usually medium because you can reach twenty to thirty people in a room for a small-scale seminar or presentation.

Menu Option 5: Direct Mail

Ian: This means writing a letter directly to potential clients. One of the advantages of direct mail is that it allows you to reach exactly who you want and write to them (assuming your mail gets through) rather than hoping they'll be at an event you'll attend or you happen to be introduced to them. Direct mail does work if you get a high-quality targeted mailing list and you can produce a compelling letter. Typically, you're much better off writing a well-written personal letter to get an introduction. Brochures and fliers, those sorts of things, do not really work with senior executives for a service as personal as coaching.

Like the offer you might make in a public speaking presentation, direct mail often works best as a lead-in to offering something of value rather than as a direct pitch for you to come and talk to them about working together. If you've written a book you can offer a copy of that in your letter, or you can ask for an informational interview, which we're going to talk about shortly. For a coach, direct mail is often a way of making first contact for follow-up rather than to get a sales meeting.

Direct mail does not usually have a very high impact. You're certainly not going to get someone to hire you as a coach based on the strength of a letter alone. You're much more likely to get something that leads to further follow-up. But the nice thing about direct mail is that the reach can be high. If you've got the budget and you can find the names and addresses of potential clients, then you can write to them and reach a lot of them. Just expect a very low return rate - a half percent or one percent of people taking action as a result of a letter. Since the rate of return is so low, you want a reasonable budget to be able to write to as many people as possible and get a decent number of responses. The benefit of direct mail is that it allows you to reach some people you couldn't reach in other ways. It's an interesting approach you might want to consider adding to your armory.

Suzi: If you haven't built your own list, you're going to have to buy one from a reputable source. Then you'll need to spend money to buy a large enough list, and make sure it's a database that's kept current. Don't make the mistake of buying an outdated list. With direct mail there is always going to be a percentage of the list that won't get the direct mail piece for one reason or another. The chance of the piece being thrown away before it even gets to the person you're trying to reach is pretty high.

Menu Option 6: Telemarketing

Ian: Telemarketing, or cold calling, probably doesn't have a great return on investment for coaches. Cold calling, of course, is calling potential clients on the phone with whom you have no relationship or introduction or previous contact and trying to get a meeting with them.

Like direct mail, it's highly dependent on the quality of the contact list. If you want to get a high-quality contact list, then you have to pay for it. And the truth is that these days, even with a high-quality list, you're unlikely to get through to an executive on the telephone. Firstly, you have to get through the gatekeepers. It's difficult enough to get through the gatekeepers if you have a warm call. It's even more difficult going cold. If they don't need your service right now, chances are you'll never get through.

If you are trying to use cold calling, a better approach than trying to get a sales meeting directly is to try to get a meeting to ask for advice from them or to do some research with them. Another idea is to request a meeting to share some useful information with them like some benchmarking you've just done or some useful case studies you could provide them. From there you can build a relationship, which could eventually lead to a sales discussion.

Cold calling requires persistence and a thick skin. It's very difficult. Many people who try cold calling give it up because the rate of rejection is high and it can be very demoralizing.

Suzi: One strategy is that if you have the direct dial number of the executive in question, try calling early in the morning (7 a.m.) or after hours (around 6 or 7 p.m.) because their gatekeeper probably works from 9 to 5 or from 8 to 6. If you're calling the direct dial before the gatekeeper is in, oftentimes you'll find the executive already at work in order to have quiet time before the day's meetings day begin. Or they may stay late to wrap things up. Trying before or after regular business hours is one strategy that's effective for reaching the actual executive.

Another strategy is to take the long view of befriending the gatekeeper. The more you befriend the gatekeeper, the better. You could even offer pro-bono coaching services to the gatekeeper. The gatekeepers run the world with some of these executives. They handle their calendar, they handle what the executive pays attention to, and they also have valuable information that can be extremely useful to you in figuring out the best way to approach and serve the client in question.

Ian: We've used the word gatekeeper because that's a commonly used term. But actually that's not a great word to use because it can negatively impact your mindset towards this influential person. More often than not, the executive assistant of a senior executive is an influencer of that executive. It's very easy to say, "I need a strategy for getting past the gatekeeper," but if you swap that word for *influencer*, you wouldn't find yourself saying, "How can I get past the influencer?" Instead you're likely to say, "How can I make a great impression and befriend that influencer so that positive messages get through to the executive?"

Suzi: Once you've established trust, the influencer will often share unsolicited and valuable information with you, such as the availability of the executive or even some of the things that are happening in the organization that the executive assistant is privy to given their role. I have often found that these executive assistants are really the best place to leverage your best relationship skills because it helps you serve your executive client better. You can become a partner with the influencer in making sure the executive's needs are met.

Ian: As an example of the insight you can get from a good executive assistant, author Andrew Sobel often tells a story about a consultant working with a very senior executive. Whenever he came to meet the executive for business development or relationship-building purposes, he would come in with all sorts of slides and presentations to share with the executive. At one point, the executive assistant took him aside afterwards and said, "He really values the meetings he has with you." The coach responded by saying, "Yeah, I know that. I come in really prepared with my slides and give him a valuable presentation." And she said, "No, no, no. He values the *discussions* he has with you, the slides he just considers the price he has to pay to have that discussion." That was a valuable bit of coaching that the executive assistant gave to the consultant, and it showed him that he wasn't running his meetings in the best way for that client.

Suzi: Executive assistants know how to communicate with your client. They can be your best partners in bringing forth the best that you have to offer.

Ian: Very often, the very first person an executive speaks to after they've had a session with you will be the executive assistant. So if your coaching doesn't have the desired impact, the first person to know about it may be the executive assistant, who might be able to give you some useful feedback.

Suzi: The executive assistant can particularly help when it comes to the calendar. I have found that when you have an alliance with the person who's handling the calendar for the executive, your meetings don't get rescheduled as often.

Ian: Cold calling is more effective when used in combination with other approaches. We talked earlier about using referrals. Ideally, referrals are going to get you a direct connection, an introduction from someone to a target client for you, but it could well be that the referrer isn't quite ready to phone up the potential client and make the introduction themselves, but they are willing for you to use their name. If you then make a call and say, "John Smith suggested I call you," you're far more likely to get through than if you didn't have a mutual acquaintance to mention. At that point it becomes warm calling.

Typically, the impact of pure cold calling is quite low. The reach can be medium. You can make a lot of calls in a day if you want, though can be a bit soul destroying for you if you make a lot of calls and get a lot of rejection.

Menu Option 7: Traditional Advertising

Suzi: Advertising is not generally effective for executive coaching, which is a high-trust, high-touch service, because advertising is the opposite.

Ian: Advertising can work to raise awareness, but it would have to be in a specialist publication rather than the general media, which is very expensive to advertise in. Like some of the other forms of marketing, advertising is best used as a starting point. You might be able to use advertising to get people to a seminar, which you then use to get people into a one-to-one discussion. But in general, advertising is not something I've ever seen work effectively for us, and there are better choices for your resources. You may get a call from an ad executive who might try and tell you that you could reach thousands in your target market by advertising in their magazine, or on their airline, or their radio show, but in all honesty, we haven't really seen it work. Be wary and do your research.

Typical impact, because it's an advert, is very low. Reach could be high at high cost, because you can get a message in front of many, many thousands of executives, but it just wouldn't have that much impact.

Suzi: Again, manage your expectations because that's not going to directly lead to one-on-one executive coaching.

Ian: That's right, the advert itself is not going to lead immediately to a client contact. It's much easier to build the high level of trust needed if you're doing executive coaching through avenues other than advertising.

Menu Option 8: Public Relations

Ian: Similar to advertising, is public relations, or PR, which essentially means engineering mentions in the press. If you have something newsworthy to share or if something breaks in the news in an area that you're working, or there's something interesting going on in a particular industry you're working, then you could potentially add commentary on that and it might be reported. PR works if your potential clients are paying attention to the media that you get mentioned in. If you get mentioned in a certain trade publication but your clients never read that, it's going to have no impact. To get PR to work, you have to invest in PR and obviously sometimes you may have to pay a PR person for that.

A PR technique that's being used increasingly is what's known as "newsjacking." That's where you monitor the news for breaking stories in your area and then you contact relevant journalists to add your commentary in an area that you're an expert on or you know about in some way. Like Suzi was mentioning before with the advert, if you happen to focus in a particular niche, you're an expert. If you have a book, then you could often get mentioned in the press by adding commentary to something that breaks as a story. If you speak at an event or you've written an article or you have some great client results that they're willing to talk about, then you can try and get PR out of it, which can help raise your profile. Typically, for me, PR is a bonus, rather than a frontline strategy.

Suzi: Just to be clear, when we're talking about this kind of PR, we're talking about the traditional media outlets. We're not talking about social media, which we're going to get into later. This is the more formal public relations where you typically are working with a professional in that arena who's seeking to get you visibility in the major media outlets - television, radio, well known publications, and newspapers.

Ian: Typically, the impact of one individual piece of PR is low. The way PR works is that your name becomes better known as the mentions of your name gradually accumulate in the appropriate sectors.

Menu Option 9: Writing Articles

Ian: Much like making presentations, writing articles is about demonstrating your expertise. Having your article published can be a very effective credibility builder if your target clients actually read it in a prestigious publication. It works best to raise your profile and credibility if you're doing it regularly. Clients see your name mentioned in multiple places. Wherever they turn, you happen to be. That can have an impact on their perception of you. The only problem is that articles don't provide a direct call to action. Unless you can persuade the publication or website to allow you to have a little bio at the bottom where you provide an offer for people to contact you for a free white paper for example, then you are just raising your credibility.

Suzi: You want to have a balance of places where you publish articles. This is about reach. Do you want to have a certain number of articles that are in trade publications?

A certain number online or on blogs? You want to have a good mix of where you're posting your articles. You also want to take some of the ones that are published in the more credible publications and get nice glossy finished reprints that include the publication name. For example, if you managed to get something in *Harvard Business Review*, you want to make sure you give the glossy cover of the magazine that it appeared in and a glossy reprint of your article. You can then send that to clients or leave it with prospective clients when you're meeting with them for the first time, because that adds to your credibility in case they missed the publication when it came out.

Ian: In this case, combining article writing with direct mail to reach out to potential clients is much more credible than just sending them a letter.

Suzi: Or you use it as a "leave behind" when you meet them or put it on the chairs when you do a presentation. These are some of the ways that these menu items start to work together.

Ian: If we're just talking about articles themselves, the impact is typically pretty low per person who reads it. It's good for credibility but not good for getting you directly into contact with potential clients. The reach can be very high, and obviously it depends on the publication's circulation and target audience.

Menu Option 10: Informational Interviews

Ian: Informational interviews are a strategy that I first learned from your book, Suzi. It's really just a meeting with a potential client or other contact to get advice, feedback, and insights. You schedule a short meeting with someone, perhaps twenty minutes, and you use the time to ask important questions that you really want to know the answer to.

You can use this when you're just starting out in your coaching business or moving into a new area. Or you can do it on an ongoing basis. It's so powerful because while it's providing you with information, it is also building relationships with potential clients or potential referrers. And, of course, people are much more likely to agree to a short informational interview than to a sales meeting.

Suzi: An informational interview is a powerful tool that you can use anytime. It's a great vehicle for requesting and receiving small nuggets of wisdom or mentorship from somebody. It's a tool that I teach my executive clients because it's something that they can use inside their organizations or in their industries because it's a great way to establish and build relationships and to create some visibility for yourself.

In the case of our executive clients, I'll often have them think of some strategic influencers or key stakeholders in their success that they need to have a deeper relationship with. For us, as coaches in the business development process, it's a powerful way to gather information about the executive's needs, the organization and its challenges, and the industry they're in. If you're targeting a particular industry and you become known in those circles, you might want to do a series of informational interviews, gather data on a particular industry trend, and then write an article about that, which you can then use as a leave behind or as a direct mail piece to your potential clients.

Informational interviews are a safe way to get in front of some of these people because you're not selling anything. There's no commercial exchange; it's just, "Hey, can I pick your brain for a few minutes on x or y or z?" It's also powerful to do informational interviews with other coaches who are succeeding in the arenas in which you want to succeed. Find experienced successful coaches who are making a living doing what you want to do and conduct informational interviews with them to find out how they think about it, how they approach their clients, what their pricing structure is, what business models they've found to be most successful, or anything else you want to know. Informational interviewing is a great tool that can be leveraged in many ways.

Ian: It is amazing how much you can build credibility simply by asking questions. If your questions are smart, you build rapport and the interviewee realizes you know what you're talking about. It's remarkable that a situation in which you are asking for information rather than delivering it can make you look so bright! Often, a happy by-product of a successful informational interview is that you may end up on the shortlist for a call from that person down the road, or at least a referral from them.

Suzi: The kind of data that you gather in that informational interview then gives you a nugget of something with which to come back for a sales conversation later, if appropriate.

Ian: Yes, and I think that's one of the key outcomes. It's critical to respect the nature of the meeting. If you agreed to twenty minutes for you to pick their brain and that's the context in which they come to the meeting, you can't switch to sales mode in the meeting unless they really ask you to, and essentially drag it out of you. Twisting it around to sales without a direct request about how you might be able to help won't sit right with the executive. It would be legitimate, however, to contact them sometime later and say, "You know, I was thinking about what you said about x, and it might make sense for us to discuss that further..." and that could lead to a sales meeting.

Suzi: I had an informational interview with a publisher when my first book was about to come out. I had written the manuscript and decided I didn't have the stomach for going through the publishing process and all the rejections that I had heard would come with that. I didn't have a literary agent, and I knew I wanted to get the book out there, so I was researching what it would take to sell it to a publisher if I wanted to go that route. One of the things I decided to do in my data gathering was an informational interview with a publisher. In the course of that interview, about twenty minutes into it, he said, "I'd be interested in publishing your book." I said, "No, thank you. That's not the point of this call. I want to find out about your process and how you do what you do and what you look for in new authors." He says, "Yes, I know. Tell me about your book." I said, "No, I'm not prepared to pitch my book. This is not why I'm here." By the third time he asked, he was getting a little angry with me and said, "Tell. Me. About. Your. Book." At which point I figured I'd better comply. That's how I ended up getting published. He argued with me a bit about my topic and premise, decided I knew what I was talking about, and he took a risk on whether or not I could actually write well. The publisher picked it up and sent me a contract within days, and it was all from the informational interview.

Ian: Completely refusing to sell might be going a bit far. But generally you want to go in with the spirit of gathering information and taking advantage of the wonderful opportunity this person has provided.

Executives are often quite generous about giving their time because many have had experiences in which others helped them as they rose through the ranks. Just don't abuse that kindness and generosity by sneaking in a sales pitch.

Typically in terms of impact, informational interviews can be high. They are a great opportunity to build the credibility, trust, and the relationship that's needed to get someone almost ready to hire you. The reach depends on how many you want to do, so it could be low if you just decide to do a handful.

Suzi: Prior to starting my coaching business, I spent six months doing 150 informational interviews, but I didn't set out to do that many. I started out with three because I was searching for information about how I could transition from my previous career into coaching. I was looking for the connecting points. One of the questions I asked in every informational interview was, "Is there anyone else that you would recommend that I talk to about this because I'm trying to figure out what my next steps are?" I followed up on every single one of those referrals, and that's how I interviewed 150 people in six months. I got my entire coaching business started that way, and learned valuable insights about how networking really works.

Follow the 80–20 rule in the interview. You want to get the other person talking 80 percent of the time. If it's a fifteen- or twenty-minute informational interview, you don't want to spend ten or fifteen minutes of that time talking about yourself. The focus is all about them.

Menu Option 11: Websites

Ian: We're going to look at a few online approaches, but we'll start with websites. First and foremost, understand that no matter who you are, potential clients (or those that advise and influence them) are going to check out your website. So at a bare minimum, your website has to be credible, it has to say what your services are, the type of results you get, and who you work with so that users can determine whether you could be a match for them.

There are a few critical components for your website. Ideally you'll have testimonials on there from people saying what a great job you've done and the results they've received from working with you. You will also want to have some content that's regularly updated to demonstrate your expertise. That could be articles, blog posts, videos, or a podcast - any kind of valuable content that demonstrates your credibility.

Valuable content is going to help boost your website in searches, and it will build your credibility once people land there. It will also increase the chances that other websites will link to yours, which is another way to improve your search-engine ranking. If you want to use your website in this way, you'll need to build your understanding of how this process works and put some investment into generating traffic - getting the right people to your website.

Getting an initial contact through your website is only going to work if people are actively searching and looking online for the sort of problems that you help people solve. It does not necessarily have to be your target client exactly doing the searching. Sometimes an executive might say to someone on his or her team, "Go and look for this for me. Can you find me a shortlist of five people who do this?" In that case it's not necessarily the person who's going to be your client doing the searching. You do need someone to be actively searching.

Just like with in-person marketing, you're going to need to follow up. It's rare that someone will visit your website and then hit your contact form to hire you on that very first visit. You'll need some form of follow up just like you do with many of the other forms of marketing. A good way to do that is email marketing. Visitors sign up for regular emails from you, and then you're able to do follow-up emails with them to build credibility and trust.

Suzi: I think the bottom line about your website is that it should speak directly to your client and their issues and needs rather than being just a brochure about how great you are. Use your client's language and frame it to speak directly to the visiting client.

Ian: You really do want your ideal client (or the person searching on their behalf) to say, "Yes, this is for me. I'm in the right place," when they visit your website. When users don't immediately get the impression that they'll get something useful from the website, that it's designed for people just like them, then they click away pretty quickly.

Typically, the reach of the website depends on the traffic you're getting. The impact can be medium. It's not the same as being in person and talking to face-to-face, but depending on the resources, testimonials, videos, and other tools on your website, it can make quite a significant impact.

These days, potential clients are going to check out your website. If it looks very dated, if it looks amateurish, or like your teen-age child put it up for you, it's not going to create the right impression for an executive. You'd be surprised how many coaches to this day build their websites on the cheap. The website represents you and the quality of service you provide. If it looks cheaply done, it will communicate shoddy service at best, and at worst, it will indicate that you are not successful enough to afford a professional website.

Suzi: You also want to make sure that your site can be found on a quick Google search. It has to have keywords and search engine optimization sufficient to be on Google's front page. It's worth looking into being a Google Plus member because Google likes to put things higher up on Google that it already has information for and connections to.

Ian: Another issue to keep in mind is that you need to be easily findable by someone searching for your name. And then ideally, you want to be found by people searching for the type of problems you solve, the issues you address, or even something like executive coaching in the town or city you reside in.

Suzi: You also want to be found for the common misspellings of your name. If you don't own a website that is your-name-dot-com, make sure you purchase that domain simply to protect yourself from others using your name in ways that you wouldn't want.

Ian: These things can happen accidentally too. It happens to be the case that I share a name with the ex-deputy prime minister of Canada and a relatively famous photographer in New Zealand who's recently become much more famous because he was the official photographer for all of the Lord of the Rings films and the Chronicles of Narnia films. As a result, my name started going down the search engine rankings so I had to put effort into even being ranked for my own name. That was eye- opening.

Menu Option 12: Social Media

Ian: There are many ways of using social media. One of the first things to keep in mind, however, is that various social media sites won't give you much value if your clients aren't actually on there. For instance, not as many executives are on LinkedIn as it sometimes seems. Some of them are on LinkedIn in name only, perhaps because their assistant put their profile on because someone said they should have a LinkedIn profile.

In my experience, the best use of LinkedIn for finding and connecting with potential clients is to boost referrals. One of the ways to do that effectively is if you know exactly who to be referred to. Then you can say to a client or contact, "I noticed on LinkedIn that you know John Smith of Smith and Company. How do I go about getting in touch with him?" It works much better than asking more generically if he or she knows anyone in a particular industry or company. That way your contact doesn't have to go through the thought process themselves to figure out who to introduce you to.

You can use the advanced search facility on LinkedIn and search for certain job titles, or you can search people by name if you'd like to get introduced to them, or you can search by company name, by sector, by geography, and so forth. If you pay for the premium LinkedIn subscription, you can search by company size, so you can make sure the search is restricted to larger organizations where obviously someone is an executive rather than just a small business owner, which is probably not going to be a good target for you. That will bring you back a list of people who fit those criteria, and it will also show you any common connections you have. If you look for your "second order connections," the people who you know that also know this person, then you can ask that person for a referral or an introduction or even just ask them for some advice on who that person is, what they might be interested in, what their challenges are, and the best way to go about contacting them.

Using LinkedIn in that way, to find the people who could be potential clients for you and then looking to see if there's anyone you know who knows them so you can get a warm introduction is perhaps the method of using LinkedIn that will deliver the highest impact. The other way is to look at the profiles of your contacts who you feel confident will give you a good introduction or a good referral and see who they know. Very often you'll be surprised at how well connected they are.

One of the wonderful things about social media is it makes connections between people visible, and often it's surprising who your contacts know who actually would be a great contact for you or a great potential client.

Suzi: Another valuable use of LinkedIn is to pay attention to the recommendations feature because people tend to trust and value the recommendations that they see in LinkedIn more so than the ones that they will see on your website. The recommendations on your website were posted by you, and you could potentially have manipulated them to your advantage. Recommendations about you on LinkedIn allow people to click through and investigate the person who made the recommendation. It's even better if the recommendation is someone who's linked to them either first or second tier because they feel it's a more credible and trustworthy recommendation. If you don't have any recommendations on LinkedIn yet, go and request the people that know your work to write one for you.

Another key point about LinkedIn is that it's very well optimized for search engines. LinkedIn invests a lot of money in that, which saves you from investing large amounts on SEO for your own site. If you're careful to put your keywords in your summary description and you've completed your profile in a way that demonstrates what you want to be found for, then it's going to help you as people search online for a source to help them with their needs. It will help you show up higher up in their search.

The other way I enjoy using LinkedIn is when I'm about to meet with someone for a networking conversation. If I'm meeting someone for coffee or lunch for the first time, whether it's a prospective client or a just a colleague that I'm meeting, I'll look on LinkedIn to see who we know in common. Sometimes there are five or six people we know in common and they are related to the same community and that makes sense. Sometimes it's not logical; there may be a completely random connection we have in common and that will be a conversation starter, like "Oh, I saw on LinkedIn that we both know John Doe. How on earth do you know John Doe?"

It makes the world much smaller and creates a different level of relatedness with the person because instead of just pure curiosity, now you've got a connection.

Ian: Suzi made a good point about the profiles. Always make sure your LinkedIn profile is very client focused - what you would want any potential client to see and to think and to read about you. A lot of people on LinkedIn make it sound like a résumé. Obviously if you're hunting for a new job then a résumé format is great, but most of us aren't looking for a new job. We're looking for clients. So we need to make sure that what people see in our profile is attractive to clients. That means being very clear what we do, what value we bring to potential clients, who we work with, and maybe some links to examples of the presentations we've done, awards we've won, clients we serve.

Unfortunately in the latest version of LinkedIn, recommendations are less visible and you can't really move them up on your profile. There are the endorsements of course, but those are a bit of a game. LinkedIn is pushing the endorsement feature so it appears high up on your profile. If a lot of people endorse you for executive coaching (or leadership or whatever you want to be known for), that can impact how visitors to your profile view you.

Another possibility is to contribute to groups on LinkedIn. Although many people recommend becoming known as an expert using LinkedIn groups, I know very few people who that's really worked for when it comes to connecting with executives. Senior executives don't typically use chat or discussion forums, even on LinkedIn. You might build a good reputation with your peers or with other people who are influential, but I would advise being cautious because LinkedIn groups can take a lot of time.

Suzi: If you're going to go that route, make sure you're answering questions and not asking them, because asking them takes even more time because then you have to respond to everyone who has answered.

Ian: LinkedIn impact can be medium. It can be high impact if you're using it to identify people to personally refer you. The reach is medium as well because it's online, so you can reach a lot of people you wouldn't be able reach otherwise. But finding connections with individuals is the real value.

The other big network on social media when it comes to professionals is Twitter. Here again potentially you could use Twitter to connect with potential clients.

As with LinkedIn, Twitter is not going to work to get you connected to potential clients if your target clients aren't using Twitter. Many executives are not active Twitter users, but some are. I know, for example, a very senior managing partner in a large law firm, he's in his sixties right now, the sort of person you'd have thought wouldn't be a big Twitter user, but he is forever tweeting about football, the restaurants he likes, his vacations, music, and so forth. So if you connect with him on Twitter, you find out about what he's interested in and you can begin to build a bit of a relationship with him as if you were meeting him face-to-face in some kind of a social situation. So you'll have to experiment a bit and use the various Twitter search tools and directories to find out if your clients are on Twitter or not.

To find people, there are the basic tools built in to Twitter. Then there are external services like FollowerWonk.com, which gives you a more advanced way of searching

Twitter bios and tweets. If you find that potential clients are on Twitter, then monitor their activity. See what they're talking about. If it's appropriate, engage in a discussion with them. Retweet the things that they are tweeting. Send them a message and a link to an article you think might be useful for them. Using Twitter effectively is really about the normal human engagement you would do if you met them in the real world.

Of course the key is to eventually convert that online relationship to a live contact. No one is going to hire you as a coach simply based on interacting with you on Twitter. You've got to use it as a starting point so that when the relationship is strong enough, you can suggest having a phone call or grabbing a coffee if you're based near each other. Then you can begin to build the relationship properly offline.

One way to use Twitter is just to try and generate traffic to your website by tweeting links to your articles. This will get you a certain number of people clicking those links.

Suzi: Twitter is a great place to go to back to the mindset of "be of service." People often ask questions on Twitter, so you can answer questions. Another act of service to keep in mind is reminding clients to monitor Twitter for their brands and for their organization because if they are not, then they could be missing out on potential customer service opportunities there as well.

Ian: Twitter can be a nice way of just keeping in touch with clients and potential clients once you've already made that in-person connection. I have some clients who do this in just five or ten minutes a day. They have a private Twitter list of their clients and potential clients that no one else can see. The list allows them to only look at the tweets from those on the list rather than seeing the usual stream of Twitter activity. If those on the list tweet something interesting, they will retweet it or tweet back to them, and they will try to engage them in conversation. That's an efficient way to keep in touch with someone. It's acceptable if someone tweets something, a funny joke, to tweet them back and say, "Haha, have you heard this one?" sort of thing. You can have pretty casual conversations. If you sent an email or phoned them up to do that, it wouldn't feel normal because it's a trivial sort of thing but it works on Twitter.

Twitter lets you build those casual relationships with more people than you can manage if you were trying to do it all face-to-face. By using private lists on Twitter or maybe a CRM system that brings a social media feed in, you can manage many more relationships. It's not going to replace face-to-face communication. It's just another way of having more contact with people to build a relationship.

Twitter can have a medium impact for those people you do it with consistently. And if a lot of your potential clients are active Twitter users, the reach can be medium.

Menu Option 13: Webinars and Teleseminars

Ian: Perhaps you have heard Suzi and I do a webinar or a teleseminar before. Using online presentations and talks is just like doing a live presentation. You're showcasing your capabilities and getting across some of your personality. The key thing with a webinar or teleseminar is that your target audience has to be online enough to find out about the webinar, to sign up for it, and to attend online. If your target clients are the sorts of people who wouldn't know how to do that, then it's probably not going to work for you. But if they are, you can reach a lot more of them and it's more convenient than a live presentation.

Just like with public speaking, you have to be able to deliver a great talk, and you have to have that offer to create opportunities for follow-up. Since there is no opportunity for people to approach you in person after a webinar or teleseminar, the offer is especially critical. An offer can simply be something like this: "For people who would like to take this further and learn how they can improve performance in this area in their organization, go to this site, fill in the contact form, and I'll get back to you and we'll set up a one-to-one discussion over the telephone." In that way you can lead the webinar into a one-to-one discussion. Or you can lead the webinar into signing up to get a copy of your book or a white paper, and then you can begin nurturing the relationship via email. Again, a webinar won't directly lead to being hired, but it can lead to relationships.

Suzi: What's nice about a webinar or a teleseminar is that it can be leveraged in many different ways after it's over. When you do a live talk, you get off stage and you're done. But when you do a webinar or teleseminar, you have a recording and you can leverage that recording on your website, and you can offer it as a direct email piece to your prospective clients. It can become a product that you then beef up with workbooks or charts or add transcripts or bonus features, and then you can sell it. Look for other ways to leverage it once you've recorded it.

Ian: A webinar provides a medium impact. You will always get more impact from a face-to-face presentation, but you can often reach many more people with a webinar. My usual audience for a live presentation is between ten and thirty. It is only occasionally a hundred or more, but with a webinar, I can have one or two hundred people or more. And, of course, it can be a lot more convenient for you and your attendees.

Next Steps

Suzi: We've talked about a lot of different menu options, but don't feel like you have to do all of them. A better strategy is to have a balance of depth and breadth in your approach. If you're networking constantly, pick two or three other approaches that resonate for you and try those. If they don't yield fruit after three to six months, then switch to another one.

Consistency is an important factor in all of these, however. For instance, if people who visit your website convert to seeking your newsletter and sign up for it, then they're going to expect it to be delivered. That also helps build credibility and rapport.

Ian: This really applies to everything. If you're going to use presentations, you've got to be out doing a lot of them. If you're networking, you've got to be doing it all the time. If you do the website and email like me, it's no good just sending an email newsletter three times and then dropping it. People expect an email from me every few days, and I've been doing that for over five years. You want to test things out for three to six months to determine whether it's working, but once you know it's working, then you have to do it consistently.

Suzi: Another trend nowadays is a Daily Tips sort of email. I have a colleague who sends out a very short daily email to those who have signed up to receive his Daily Tips, and it is a two-to-three sentence bit of content or quote. What's nice about it is that it gets his branding in front of interested parties every single day at the same time of day. He builds trust and credibility with each daily missive and has gotten clients from it directly, as people share it with others who then sign up.

Ian: In the next chapter, we're going to go in depth into a combination of a couple of these approaches but largely relying on some of that face-to-face referral-based marketing that we call the **coach approach to finding new clients**. That will form the core of your marketing and give you the best results. Once you are armed with a full understanding of the coach approach, then come back to this chapter and the workbook and add in a few of the menu options from this chapter.

Suzi: Don't try to add them all in at one time. You can just start with one, master that one, and then maybe move on to trying another one. Manage what works best with your style and your susceptibility to becoming overwhelmed.

Ian: Better to be master of one than mediocre at three or four.

Toolbox:

Checklist for Action: Marketing Idea Kick-starters

Use this action checklist to kick-start your marketing activities if you don't know where to start or if you just want to get your marketing progress unstuck.

1. Determine if your priority is retention, acquisition, or reacquisition. (*Retention* is growth, maintenance, and reassessment of new and existing buyers. *Acquisition* is seeking and contracting with prospective buyers. *Reacquisition* is rekindling lost, discouraged, or past-successful buyers.)
2. Create or update collateral materials (logo, business identity, cards, letterhead, etc.).
3. Website development: Create or update your website.
4. Write a column, articles, books, or create products.
5. Explore direct means of outreach to your target market: direct mail, promotional offers, survey/research, invitational seminars/events, advertising, public relations.
6. Explore indirect means of getting your message out through intermediaries: speaking engagements, teaching opportunities, writing and publishing, association involvement, survey/research activity, media engagements, pro bono work, sponsoring programs/events.
7. Determine fifteen to twenty ways you will generate leads.
8. Consider email and web campaigns.
9. Offer free bonuses, free downloads, and free reports as ways to capture the email addresses of interested parties and grow your list.
10. Link your products and events.
11. Vary your offering so that you have entry level price points and premium products.

Marketing Menu and Marketing Approaches Worksheet

The marketing menu is a guide to the most effective marketing strategies available for executive coaches. It is meant to be used as a set of options to choose from. We don't recommend using all of these approaches at once. To help you determine which approaches are best for you, review the options while assessing the impact and reach you are seeking as well as what you know will work best with your ideal clients. It is also important to consider your own personality, comfort level, capabilities, and preferences.

Below you will see each item on the marketing menu discussed in this chapter.
Once you have reviewed the list of options, you will be ready to use the Marketing Approaches Worksheet. The worksheet allows you to rate each method, its impact, its reach, and your comfort level/ ability. We've suggested rating each method High, Medium, or Low in each area, but you can also give each method a set of numerical ratings on a scale of 1–10 if that suits you better.

Then give a short rationale for each rating to make sure you're rating each method objectively, having considered the impact and reach even if your comfort level is low. Keep in mind that some of these methods may be growth opportunities for you!

Marketing Menu

Existing Client Development
What is it?

- Getting more business from existing clients - working with other executives in the same or related organizations, or doing more work with the same executive.

When does it work?

- Works for pretty much all executive coaches except start-ups.

Requires

- Thinking creatively about what else you could offer and to who else.
- Courage to ask.

Typical Impact: Very high; Reach: Low

Referrals
What is it?

- Getting existing/previous clients and contacts to recommend you to new contacts.

When does it work?

- Works for pretty much all executive coaches except those who don't have an existing contact base.

Requires

- Creating clear and succinct descriptions of who you're looking to be referred to, what to look for, and what value you bring to the table.

Typical Impact: High; Reach: Low

Networking Events

What is it?

- Meeting potential clients (and referrers) face to face at events.

When does it work?

- Dependent on existence of "reachable" events/forums with a high percentage of target clients and referrers (usually rare that senior executives go to normal networking events).

Requires

- Networking skills: openness, interest in others, and ability to give clear description of what you do, how you help, and who you help.

Typical Impact: Low; Reach: Low

Public Speaking & Seminars

What is it?

- Showcasing your capabilities (and your personality) on stage.

When does it work?

- When you can speak well and you can find the right audience. If you're a good speaker, you're more likely to get to an exclusive event than as an attendee.

Requires

- Excellent speaking skills. Need strong reputation and track record to get booked for senior executive events.
- Clear next step/call to action to translate to talking to you one on one.

Typical Impact: High; Reach: Medium

Direct Mail

What is it?

- Writing directly to potential. Allows you to target exactly who you want (rather than hoping they'll be at an event you attend, for example).

When does it work?

- When you can get a high-quality, targeted mailing list, and produce a compelling letter.

Requires

- Well-written personal letter rather than a brochure/flyer.
- Often best as lead in to offering something of value rather than a direct pitch.

Typical Impact: Low-Medium; Reach: High (depending on budget)

Telemarketing/Cold Calling

What is it?

- Calling potential clients on the phone to try to get a meeting with them.

When does it work?

- Dependent on quality of contact list - and on likelihood of executive needing service in near future.

Requires

- Having something more to offer than just a pitch for your services.
- Persistence and a thick skin.

Typical Impact: Low; Reach: Medium

(Traditional) Advertising

What is it?

- Purchasing of advertising space in traditional print media/radio/TV.

When does it work?

- Could work to raise awareness of a new brand or introduce a new service. But can be very costly to use general media. Specialist press can be much more targeted if available for target prospects.
- Generally speaking, unlikely to be effective for executive coaches.

Requires

- Something to offer that's more than just a sales pitch.

Typical Impact: Very low; Reach: High (at high cost)

PR

What is it?

- Engineering mentions in press.

When does it work?

- When you have something newsworthy to share, or if you have something to add to a hot news story.
- If your potential clients pay attention to the media you get mentioned in.

Requires

- Investment in PR. Monitoring news for opportunities to add expert commentary.

Typical Impact: Low; Reach: High (depending on publication)

Articles

What is it?

- Publishing articles to demonstrate your expertise.

When does it work?

- Can be very effective as credibility builder if you can find media that are read by target clients. Works best to raise your profile and credibility if you publish regularly.

Requires

- Writing skills. Persistence to keep writing and keep contacting publications.

Typical Impact: Medium-Low; Reach: Medium-High depending on publication

Informational Interviews

What is it?

- Meeting with potential clients and other contacts to get their advice, feedback and insights.

When does it work?

- Very effective for breaking into new markets. As well as providing useful information, it builds initial relationships with potential clients and referrers.
- Executives much more likely to agree to informational interview than sales meeting.

Requires

- Genuine interest. Good interviewing skills. Courage to ask.

Typical Impact: High; Reach Low-Medium

Website

What is it?

- Using your website to get found and build credibility with potential clients.

When does it work?

- If your clients (or the people who advise them) actively search online.

Requires

- Regular creation of valuable content for your potential clients.
- Understanding and investment in generating traffic.
- Ideally, follow-up via email marketing.

Typical Impact: Medium; Reach: Depends on traffic

Linkedin

What is it?

- Use of Linkedin to find and initiate contact with new potential clients.

When does it work?

- As long as potential client clients are on Linkedin and you can find a connection to them.

Requires

- Ability to find potential clients via search.
- Common connections to ask for referrals from.

Typical Impact: Medium; Reach: Medium

Twitter

What is it?

- Using Twitter to connect with potential clients.

When does it work?

- Depends on whether target clients use Twitter (not many executives do) and on your self control!

Requires

- Searching, and connecting with potential clients. Monitoring their activity. Engaging in discussion. Converting to "live" contact.

Typical Impact: Medium; Reach: Medium

Webinars/Teleseminars

What is it?

- Using online presentations/talks to showcase your capabilities (and personality).

When does it work?

- Target audience must be online enough to sign up and to attend.

Requires

- As per public speaking - ability to deliver a great talk.
- A simple next step for attendees to engage with you one on one.

Typical Impact: Medium; Reach: Medium-High

Approach	Reach (H/M/L)	Impact (H/M/L)	My Ability/ Comfort (H/M/L)	Rationale	Y/N
Existing Client Development					
Referrals					
Networking					
Public Speaking & Seminars					
Direct Mail					
Cold Calling					
Traditional Advertising					
PR					
Articles					
Research Project					
Website - Core					
Website - SEO					
Website – Pay-Per-Click					
Linkedin					
Twitter					
Webinars/Teleseminars					
Other:					

Which Marketing Approaches Will Work Best For You?

Marketing Approaches Worksheet

CHAPTER 5
The Coach Approach to Finding New Clients

Suzi: We have looked at some of the critical mindsets required for marketing and explored the menu of options for finding new clients. Now we're going go deeper into the approach we recommend for the fastest, easiest, most comfortable route to results - the *coach approach* to finding clients - which is about leveraging your personal connections and relationships as well as your skills and training as a coach.

Phase 1: Relationship Asset Inventory

Suzi: We recommend that you start by making a list of people you know. It is the quickest method for finding potential clients. We call this taking an inventory of your relationship assets. Just see what you have in stock already. In this case we mean who you're already connected to in a sufficient relationship to ask for introductions, to ask for connections, and to ask for information. These are people you know well enough and are comfortable enough with that they will take your call or meet with you.

Sociologists tell us that on average we all have a ready-made network at our fingertips of 250 people. Have you ever considered exploring your personal numbers? Here are the steps for your relationship asset inventory:

1. List the categories in your life in which you already know people. This could be family members, religious institutions that you participate in, work, co-workers, colleagues, people in your neighborhood, people you used to go to school with, and perhaps people that your children go to school with,

past employers or past business associates, friends, associations you belong to, professional groups, and any other kinds of colleagues from past or present. You can include parents of friends of yours as well as parents of your children's friends, if appropriate. You also can consider including those who provide services to you, like your dentist or any other medical professionals, or someone who helps you in your business. Each of these are categories in your life in which you already know people.

2. Then you want to make each category a separate page and list all the people you know in each category. This takes a little time, but it's easy because these are people you already know.

3. In each category, you want to choose the three people you know best and consider those to be your networking starters. These are the top three people that you feel most comfortable going to for networking help.

4. Then set up a time to talk with your networking starters; tell them your vision and ask for theirs. Ask them who they know that you could talk to about your vision and offer people you know who could be a good contact for them. In other words, you're starting with those you know and you're asking them who they know. You're seeking to be of service to them as well as asking for what you need.

5. Then you may want to follow up. You want to seek out every person that your networking starters refer you to, and again, tell them your vision. Tell them what you're up to and ask each of these people who they know that you might talk to.

You want to continue to work this way through your network list, seeking to be of service to the people you're meeting by generously offering your network to them for whatever matters most to them. Then you want to continue with the follow up. Keep meeting people from your network starters' networks, and allow it to continue to expand. Make sure that you tell everyone you meet what you're up to in your business and in your life. Provide everyone with a clear profile of your ideal clients.

Plant some seeds for referrals. Ask for introductions. This may sound awkward, but it really is not. You might say, "Do you happen to know anybody who is x?" Or say, "Do you know anyone who needs y and could use z?" Of course you're going to fill in the x, y, z with things that are meaningful to you and what you're trying to do. Or you might say, "Do you or anyone you know ever find that you have this particular challenge?" You then highlight one of your target client's typical challenges. That will help the people you're talking to know how to recommend people to you or what kinds of people to point in your direction.

Phase 2: Working Backwards From Your Target Clients

Ian: In the first phase, we have inventoried the people we know to help move us toward the people we want to get to, our potential clients. In the next phase, we're going to go at it the other way around. We'll start off by thinking of who we'd really like to have as clients and then work our way back to the people we know who know them. Ideally we're going to meet somewhere in the middle.

Here are the steps for this second phase:

1. Start by making a list of everyone you know who is in an industry or an organization that appeals to you. List the types of businesses or organizations that you'd really like to work with. It could be Fortune 500 companies generally. It could be nonprofits, or professional service organizations: whichever are the ideal clients for you as we discussed in Chapter 1.

2. Next, list everyone you know who is connected to those organizations in some way. It could be that they work in those organizations. It could be that they provide service to those organizations. It could be that they are clients or customers of those organizations or they have friends or relatives in those organizations. Cast your net wide, but make sure you go deep too. You don't always know precisely who the people you know actually know, so make as long a list as possible about who you know who may be connected to these organizations.

3. Then prioritize that list based on who will be able to connect you to executives in the type of organizations you're targeting. It's a bit like the previous list but based not around the categories of how you know them but on who those people might be able to get you in touch with. Like before, you're prioritizing the ones who will be able to get you connected. What you'll probably do is think of the people who you feel comfortable with - those it will be easiest for you to pick up the phone and ask if they can introduce you to someone in one of your ideal organizations. If it helps you to be comfortable, you might consider writing a brief script and practicing your request. Obviously when you make the request in real life, you want it to sound as natural as possible. If you work best just with a few bullet points and notes, go from that. If you work best by scripting it and then practicing and practicing until

it sounds natural, then do that. At its most basic it is asking who they know and who they are willing to introduce you to.

Suzi: One way of looking at this is to take that list and set it up as a hierarchy. The strongest type of personal relationship that you can use is someone who can refer you with confidence - someone who knows you, knows your work, and knows the kind of results you can get for clients.

Second in the hierarchy are people who know you and like you, but haven't yet seen you in action. They've never seen your results with clients so they can't vouch for your work. Most would be willing to introduce you, but they can't sing your praises in the way the first level of contact can.

These are the sorts of people who might just pass on an email and say, "Hey, you should speak to John, he does work in just that area." Or they might be willing for you to use their name if you make a phone call to someone, and say, "Alan Smith suggested I give you a call." They can make an introduction but they can't make a strong recommendation since they haven't first-hand seen your work and its results.

The other set of people are those you know who have a strong contact base (meaning they are in a good position to introduce or recommend you) but you don't know them well enough to ask for that introduction or recommendation. The idea with this set of people is to focus on developing your relationship with them so that over time they gain the confidence to recommend you. Think about how you can get them to see the results of what you do or to see you in action so they will be able to vouch for you. Storytelling is a useful avenue towards building that awareness for them.

Finally, add on to that list the people you don't know personally yet but who are ideally placed to introduce you. For example, if you would like to work in the legal sector with executives in law firms, then add the chairperson of the local law society or professional networking organization. You don't know them, but you know of them and you know that they know a lot of the people you want to get introduced to. Think long term and create a plan for getting an introduction to that person and building your relationship with them over time.

If possible, identify the super-connectors in any community you wish to get introduced. Those are usually the best-connected individuals and often they are generous and eager to introduce you to everyone they know. Seek to be of service to the super-connectors and they will repay the favor tenfold with connections into their network.

You now have a list of various levels of people ranging from those who are ready, willing, and able to recommend you to potential clients, to people who'd be happy to make introductions, to people you have to strengthen or form relationships with.

Ian: When you do this exercise, make sure you scour all the sources you can. LinkedIn is a huge help with this. Make sure you're connected to everyone on your list on LinkedIn. Once you are connected, you can go to their profile and see who they know. What you find - the number of excellent introductions your connections can make for you - may surprise you.

Another way to use LinkedIn is the advanced search capability. It allows you to specify various criteria for people you'd like to find on LinkedIn. You can search by job title or industry sector or certain types of groups. For example, there are various legal industry groups on LinkedIn, if you join those you can specify that the people in the search results must be a member of a number of those groups as well. You can also specify a geography so you can see within fifty miles of a city, for example, or a certain post or zip code so you can try to get local clients. It will then show you a list of people who meet those criteria.

Once you've done your LinkedIn search and created a long list of people who meet your criteria, you filter that list down to show only the second order connections. This will show you the people who are connected to people who you're also connected to. And on the list it will tell you who your common connections are. Often there are quite a few if you're well connected. So by clicking on the list of common connections, you can identify whether any of those common connections would be willing to refer or introduce you. Once you know that common connection, if there are people who you already know can refer you with confidence, then you ask for that. If there are just people who can introduce you, you ask for that. If it's someone who you just know and connected to on LinkedIn but you really don't feel confident asking yet, then you work on building your relationship with them. You especially want to do that for someone whose name comes up many times as a common connection.

What you are really doing by that targeting is you are deciding who you would like as clients and then you are making that clear to people and you are finding connections to those people.

Suzi: Now when you do make a call to ask those people for referral or an introduction, it helps if you can be as specific as possible. What you want is a specific description of the role of the person you are seeking. It could be the CFO in a pharmaceutical company, a female partner in professional service firms, military and veterans that are transitioning to civilian leadership roles. Healthcare leaders, mid-level managers in tech firms, etc. You need your description to be specific enough that people can easily tell whether they know someone who fits the bill.

Ideally you've also got a list of specific individuals you'd like referrals or introductions to from your LinkedIn searches. In this case you are really giving the person you are asking something they can get hold of and easily say, "Yes, I know that person". The more you are focused your description of who you'd like to be introduced or referred to the easier it's going to be for people to make that introduction.

The other way of looking at it is not the description of ideal clients in terms of the industry, the sector, or the type of person they are, but the sort of problem they face. For instance, in this case it could be senior women leaders hitting a glass ceiling or newly promoted executives in fast-growing industries who are struggling with leadership for the first time. If you come at it from that angle, then you're directly hitting the motivation why they might want to hire an executive coach.

Ian: Of course, sometimes it's difficult to find those people just based on the description of their problem. It's easier to find people who work in a certain industry or who meet a certain demographic because those are externally visible factors whereas problems are often known only to the person suffering from them. But if you do find people who are hitting the glass ceiling, have a certain leadership problem, and so forth, then often they are much more motivated to hire someone because they have a specific problem you can help with.

When you're looking for introductions and referrals, don't forget the different roles of people we discussed earlier. Not only do you have the executives who might need coaching themselves, but you have very senior executives who might authorize coaching programs, or HR people who may introduce you to potential clients and be influential in hiring decisions. When you're looking for people to be introduced to, make sure you also consider these roles. All of them could be valuable connections.

If you're targeting people by the sector or industry they're in, then it's easier to find those potential clients but they might not have a need for a coach right now. Conversely if you are targeting a particular problem, then it's harder to find those potential clients but easier to get them to yes.

Ideally, if you can find the mix of the two that go together, then you will be in very good situation. It could be, for example, your targets are the R&D heads of pharmaceutical companies because they are typically isolated and frustrated because the sales guys get the top job. It's easy to find R&D heads of pharmaceutical companies and they all have a common leadership challenge that you are able to deal with.

This, of course, is closely related to the different factors you used to identify your niche in Chapter 2. Ideally you're looking for a decision maker with a significant problem or goal and with money to solve it that matches the skills you have in an area you have a passion for.

So by looking at your strengths, the connections you already have, all your experience, your expertise, that helps you understand the best niche for you and the sorts of people you should be connecting with.

Look at that niche: does it make sense, is it feasible, can I reach it? But also keep open to the niche "finding you" as Suzi showed from her experience. She didn't set out to target executives in law firms but that niche found her.

Remember, if you can't figure out your niche, start prospecting anyway. You will be able to refine it as you go along. Especially if you are just starting out, it can be really difficult to know which type of niche, which type of organization, which type of person you really love to work for and with whom your skills are an ideal match. All you can do is get yourself out there. Start prospecting. Start getting introductions to potential clients. Over time, you will get a much better idea of what your ideal niche is, or whether you need one at all.

Suzi: It's okay when your target changes as your passion changes, as your calling changes, or as your life experiences change. That's alright. But what Ian has been talking about, this business of creating a list of who can introduce you to whom, working on that over time and making that list stronger is always important. This is your first port of call because it is how you are going to have more success, and it will feel more comfortable than any of the other methods. We just want you to be relaxed about this process of targeting. It is just about getting going, and being in action about it.

We are not saying spend six months going in circles figuring out who your target is or doing these worksheets. Try one and see what happens. You will never really know until you get out there. It is going to keep changing. Be open to that. That's why the most perfectly simple place to start is by listing all the people you know already. Perhaps there's a niche that will emerge once you see your list, and you won't know that until you've gone through this exercise. The point of listing everyone you know is to help you find people who could be potential buyers of your services, evaluating the feasibility of your target list so that you can determine if they are actually buyers or not. Some of the worksheets we've provided at the end of the chapter (and online) can help with this.

Phase 3: Conversations

Once you have done all the listing that you can do of all the people that you are even remotely linked to, the next step is to get into scheduling conversations with each of them. Ideally you have prioritized your list according to your current level of comfort in picking up the phone and asking for a conversation or a meeting. We recommend making things easy for yourself. The folks you already know can be the beginning of expanding your potential clients because they are going to suggest connections for you. They are going to facilitate those connections either with an introduction or permission to use their name when you reach out to the new contact.

These conversations are very brief calls, five minutes or less. These are not long, pitch-your-services kinds of calls. Think of it like calling the dentist's office to schedule a dental appointment. They are quick scheduling conversations. You can also do this by email, or you can leave a voice mail. This is just a call to schedule a conversation about what you're up to and whether or not this person knows anyone in your ideal set of people and whether they are comfortable to make a recommendation or introduction for you. You are not attempting to get on the phone and convince anyone to buy anything.

Ian: If you started out by trying to make a call to a chief executive of a large organization that you didn't know, most people would really struggle with that. Focus first on the people you know who are likely to say yes to a meeting and be receptive to your request. Talk to them about your vision and where you are headed, and ask them to connect you to the right people with whom you wish to speak to get the ball rolling quickly. This will get you into the habit of networking and will bring in new contacts for you to meet.

Suzi: Once you have already connected with people who know you and can introduce you to others, it becomes much easier once you have that first meeting with a senior person you don't know. It is a way of training yourself and preparing yourself to go out into the world and be more actively speaking to people about potentially becoming your client. It is safest to start with the people you know because they are on your side. They want you to succeed, and it's going to help you to practice making the request for introductions because you are more comfortable with the people that you already know to do that. Then you start to develop that muscle and that skill and then when you start getting to people that you don't know as well, you'll still have the capability of asking for introductions. That's how you build your network. It does not have to be perfect. You don't have to say it perfectly or cleanly or have it scripted. You are just talking to people you know. It will help you to practice fine-tuning how you talk about what you do and the value of your services if you start with people you know. As I mentioned earlier, this is the process I used when I left my teaching career. I did informational interviews with 150 people, but that process started with just three people that I knew and built from there by asking them for introductions and recommendations of who else I should meet. It's an ongoing activity. This is not something to just do at the start of your business. This is something to do all along.

Ian: We've mentioned a few times that you want to share your vision with the people you meet. I find that this can be incredibly powerful, especially if your vision is more than just making a lot of money from coaching. Most people who go into coaching have a vision or goal or aspiration that is bigger than themselves. They either have a gift or talent that they want to share with the world, or some goal they want to achieve that benefits the world.

For instance, many people are attracted to coaching for nonprofits because they want to help nonprofits succeed. People like to help those who want to help others. They feel positive by supporting that vision and they will be motivated to help you succeed over and above their personal feelings toward you.

To summarize next steps for you to consider: first creating your initial relationship asset inventory and start working through the list.

Then after that (or sometimes you can overlap it), create your target list or the type of people or organizations you like to work with and work through that. As we said, they will meet in the middle.

It's okay if your list isn't perfect on the first draft, or if you identify people later and come back to them. And it's fine if you're asking for introductions to go back to some of the people you've already asked and tell them that you've now realized who you really want to focus on and it's a bit different to what you discussed with them initially.

Nobody expects you to get this perfect first time. So just get started and keep refining it. Do the exercise on an ongoing basis and that way you will keep bringing more and more potential clients into your circle of influence.

Suzi: Especially if you have hit a low on your business development, the place to return to get started, to get things moving again is always in this networking stage.

Ian: In fact, if you're an experienced coach who is going through a rocky patch and looking to invigorate your business, it can be even more powerful for you because your network is likely to be larger than a start-up coach and it's also likely to be more targeted.

You are also likely to have more senior people in your network because of the people that you coached and worked with before who can provide great introductions for you. It's just about resurrecting those relationships, getting back in touch with them and seeing where it goes from there. Nine times out of ten (or 99 times out of 100 even), people usually love to hear from you. Often we can feel a bit hesitant about getting back in touch with people we have not spoken to for a while, but as long as you have a genuine reason to reach out and you did great work for them, they'd love to hear from you.

Suzi: Just the act of making the list will help you remember other people that you might not have thought about for some time.

Ian: It's amazing how that works. You think you are carrying around in your head the complete list, but when you start writing it down on paper, it triggers more and more thoughts and ideas. Get started with making your lists, and in the next chapter we'll show you how to make those initial connections.

Toolbox

The Coach Approach to Relationship Asset Inventory

Start with who you know. The quickest method for finding potential clients is to make a list of everyone you already know. We call this taking a Relationship Asset Inventory. In essence, you will use this tool to perform an audit of the people you are already connected to in various aspects of your life. Let's see what you have in stock already. In this case we mean who you are already connected to in a sufficient relationship to ask for introductions and connections.

Identify your key contacts for the coach approach to marketing. List all the people you know in each category of your life (e.g., work, neighborhood, family, school, past employers, religious organization, community service, friends' parents, associations or professional groups, colleagues, service providers, business associates, etc.)

On the pages below, choose which category you're listing. Then list all the people you know in that category. Then mark the top three people in each category that you know the best or feel the most comfortable calling. Use the ECMBA Toolkit Checklist for Action: Networking Ideas to know what to do with the folks on these lists.

Go back through the lists and identify which organizations the people you already know are connected into. For example, you could list everyone you know in a Fortune 500 company, or everyone you know in a non-profit or government agency, or you could do it by roles. You could mark everyone on your list who holds a senior leadership or decision-making role in an organization.

Next, list everyone you know who is in any way close to or connected to the organizations you'd like to work with. Perhaps someone on your list is related to or married to someone who works at or sells products to the organizations you're most interested in.

Finally, build a list of those who you know who could help you connect to your ideal client organization and individual. From these lists, develop a call list and prioritize your calls based on the easiest calls to make. Where do you have sufficient relationship to connect and make requests? Who on your list can refer you with confidence because they know you, know your work, and know the results you produce? Who can make a personal introduction even though they have not personally experienced your work? If there are folks who could introduce you but you don't feel comfortable asking them to do so, don't put them on the top of your list.

Most importantly, get into action calling people you know and seek new relationships. To get started, list every person you know in each of the following categories:

- Through work (past employers, colleagues, etc.)
- In your neighborhood
- Through family
- In your religious organization
- Through associations and professional groups
- Friends of your parents
- Parents of your friends
- Who provide a service to you (dentist, hairdresser, etc.)
- Through your kids' schools and activities
- Who work at Fortune 500 companies
- Who work at nonprofit organizations
- Who hold a senior leadership role

If you would prefer to work on a set of worksheets, please use the ones provided in the workbook, which you can download from the Library of Professional Coaching here: http://libraryofprofessionalcoaching.com/marketing/executive-coach-marketing-resource-centre

The Coach Approach to Targeting

After completing your Relationship Asset Inventory, you are ready to start identifying which organizations or individuals you'd like to approach for conversations to explore possibilities regarding their needs and your services. This is called your target list.

Use the pages below to map out your target list of organizations, either by name or type, and by individuals within those organizations.

What is your ideal type of organization to coach in? Are you targeting Fortune 500 companies, multinational firms, professional services firms, government organizations, nonprofits? Are you targeting a specific industry or sector? Are you targeting by size of organization, or by annual revenue amount?

Who do you know who is in any way connected to that organization? You may know people who work there, who provide services to or sell products to that company, or who are married to or related to someone who works there.

List everyone you know you'd like to speak to in each client industry or sector or type of organization you can think of.

Finally, build a list of those you know who could help you connect to your ideal client organization and individual. From these lists, develop a call list and prioritize your calls based on the easiest calls to make. Where do you have sufficient relationship to connect and make requests? Who on your list can refer you with confidence because they know you, know your work, and know the results you produce? Who can make a personal introduction even though they have not personally experienced your work? If there are folks who could introduce you but you don't feel comfortable asking them to do so, don't put them on the top of your list.

Most importantly, get into action calling people you know and seek new relationships.

Make strategic choices about the people and organizations you will pursue. In marketing lingo, these are referred to as Targets. Start by making a list of your target client industry, sector, or type, (e.g. Fortune 500, Professional Services, Government, Non Profit, etc.) and then list who is connected with each particular client organization type. Or use the workbook that's available for download at [http://libraryofprofessionalcoaching.com/marketing/executive-coach-marketing-resource-centre/].

CHAPTER 6

Leading Conversations

Suzi: In this chapter, we're going to look at how to convert networking conversations into sales conversations. We want to examine that in-between stage when you're networking in any context and you want to determine if there's interest or opportunity and how to set up that next conversation to get into the sales conversations. In our experience executive coaches are prone to gloss over this in-between stage in their eagerness to get to the sales conversation or in their hurry to get through the sales conversation because it's uncomfortable. This is the very important step needed after you've found who the potential clients are, and it's about connecting with them in appropriate ways.

Ian: There are slightly different things you do depending on different situations. You may be reaching out to a contact you've not met yet, or they may be people you get referred to or they may be calling you. You'll do something slightly different in each different situation.

We're going to go through the most common of these different situations and talk about the best way of getting into the next step of getting a sales meeting or sales call with them where you figure out whether it's right for you and the potential client to be working together. There are elegant ways to transition into sales conversations.

Scratching the Surface

Ian: Imagine you're talking with someone at a social event, an actual official networking event, or somewhere else, and it begins to feel like this is someone who would need your services. Where would you normally go from there? How would you begin to broach the subject with them?

Suzi: Or even if they've actually said "Oh, I can use that" or they have said "Oh, I know somebody who could use that."

Ian: Tell you what, Suzi, that's an interesting question. Let's say you are meeting someone and they didn't say they needed your services, they haven't expressed their interest yet, but they were an executive in a corporate with the ideal client, or sounded like they would know someone, you wouldn't wait for them to come and say "Oh, that's the sort of thing I need." So, how would you go about breaking the ice to move them toward recognizing that they might need your support?

Suzi: That's a great question, because if you sit around waiting for them to say, "Oh, I need that," you're going to be waiting for a long time. An important aspect of this step in the business development process is leadership. You already know how to be a leader, so you want to lead these conversations by asking questions, which you're comfortable doing as a coach already. One tactic that works well is to lead the conversation similarly to the way you might start a coaching conversation: "What are your current challenges? What are you struggling with in your organization?" To ask a question like that you have to already have a good connection and rapport with the person and you have to have evolved the conversation to a place where they trust you enough in the networking conversation to share some of what they are dealing with and what matters to them. Once you know those things, then you can start to explore whether that person would like a thought partner or a sounding board or some brainstorming help on tactics, but just scratch the surface. Depending on the environment that you're in, you wouldn't want to spend a lot of time monopolizing that person or in that particular part of the discussion because you want to save most of that for the sales conversation. But you want to tease it out enough to explore whether it makes sense to set up another meeting. What you're listening for in that step is does it make sense for us to get together again to have a full-out conversation on whether or not it would make sense for us to work together.

Establish Rapport

Ian: Establishing rapport first is critical. You can't jump straight into a lot of questions because otherwise they won't open up. They won't tell you about their challenges and their problems until they feel they can trust you and that you'll be able to have a sensible conversation with them. It's also critical to recognize that most executives you meet aren't initially going to be thinking in coaching terms. They're thinking of the business and leadership problems and challenges they're facing, but most haven't made the leap from the problems they face to the idea that they need coaching.

They'll express their challenges with language such as: "I'm struggling with my team, I can't get them to perform" or "there always seems to be real issues when we're together" or "I don't feel confident enough in developing strategy and leading the organization." They usually know what their challenges are or their goals and aspirations are, but they haven't yet made that leap to deciding they need someone to work with them as a coach to help them.

The place to start in a discussion is the place where they are mentally. Executives are often thinking about problems, challenges, or goals, so the place to start the conversation is with asking about their goals, aspirations, and challenges. And of course if you're going to be asking about challenges, that's where you have to have established rapport first because you can't just wander in and say, "Hi, I'm Ian, what's the biggest problem you have?" because people are not going to answer that the first time they meet you.

Suzi: What you can do, however (and this is where I would encourage you to harness your own style and personality) is tap into your natural curiosity and ask a lead-in question. For example, if I've met someone and we've done the basic chit-chat and they told me they have a leadership role, I might say something like, "Oh wow, what do you find to be the most difficult part about being a leader in today's economy?" or "What do you find to be the hardest part of being a leader?" That's the language I would use. I wouldn't necessarily use a more specific coaching language like, "What's your greatest challenge?" or "What's keeping you up at night?" It's too soon to ask that, but I do go with curiosity within the networking context. The goal is to honor the space that you're in as well as your natural style.

Ian: What often works for me is starting to talk about the positive side. What are you trying to achieve? What are your big goals for this year? Talking about aspirations and goals is less risky territory than immediately jumping into problems. Of course, once you've asked about aspirations and goals, you can say, "Well, where are you on that today? How are you doing with that?" At that point they may say something like, "Actually, I'm really struggling to hit that goal." That gives you an opening to discuss the problem itself.

It's not that you're kind of trying to trick them into telling you what their problems are, it's just conversationally appropriate to talk about goals and aspirations first rather than jumping straight into problems. That's what works for me at least. Other people may be more blunt in style and jump in straight away.

Asking Questions, Casting Hooks

Ian: Another good strategy is to "throw out a hook." If you introduce yourself by describing, for example, that you work with leaders who have challenges motivating their team, then that might be enough to lead someone to ask you more about that if they have a need in that area. If someone is already asking you to tell them more about that topic, it indicates there may be something more there to discuss, they are interested enough, perhaps, for the next conversation.

Suzi: That's the point: to look at what do you do when they've expressed an interest and to be conversationally appropriate in the context of where you are. You'll rarely jump to a sale at this point. Keep in mind that the next step is likely to be a next conversation to set up. If you're at a networking or social event as we've proposed, it's also appropriate to share if you have a specialization in what you do as an executive coach. I recommend asking a question that leads down the path to your specialty. If, for example, your specialty is helping to navigate an organization's internal politics, you might say, "Do you or anyone you know ever struggle with how to navigate the politics of your organization? Do you ever find that the politics get in the way of what you are doing?" Really what you are doing is data gathering. You're not necessarily opening up a sales conversation at that moment, but you're exploring around the edges of whether or not they would have a need for your specialty.

Respecting No

Ian: If they say no, then you move on to other things but if they say, "Actually, yes," it's a way of getting into a more specific conversation about an area you can help with. You may have had conversations with aggressive salespeople where they ask you if you're interested in their product or service and you say "no", and then they come at it again later, like a terrier grabbing onto your leg that won't let go. You don't want to be that person! Respect the "no."

Suzi: We coaches love to reframe our mindsets and help our clients to do that as well. We often are raised to believe that no is a form of rejection, but the reframe I will offer us all as executive coaches is that no is a gift. There's enormous value in the no, and we should try to get people to say as quickly as possible because a no is clear. Don't fear the no as you approach these conversations. The minute someone says "no", it's a super clear end to that line of inquiry. And there's a gift in that because you can then stop pursuing that line of thought with that person, you can then explore other avenues if that makes sense to do so, or you can just return to the general human connection part of the conversation and then quickly move on to someone else who could be a potential actual client. So it's almost like we want to drive to the "no" sooner in the process rather than later and not view it as a rejection and view it instead as "Thank you, this is great, and now I know not to keep trying different buttons here and I'm going to go find somebody else." So viewing "no" as a gift is what I would offer as a reframe for everyone to try on and thus to not be avoiding the "no" or fearing the "no" which is often how we approach this conversation.

Ian: Indeed and then you end up dancing around, each trying to be polite to each other without actually saying "no" that you end up wasting each other's time which is not in anyone's interest. Of course there could be other ways in which you could be valuable to that person. They might actually have a different need that you may not address yourself but you might know someone you can refer them or introduce them to who might be able to talk to them about that particular issue or challenge.

However, having said that, something to consider when you hear no is simply that the timing may not be right just now. In that situation you want to preserve the relationship with that person if they fit your ideal client criteria because there's nothing to say that in two months, three months, six months or a year's time, they won't be ready for a sales conversation.

Suzi: So, we've discovered how to move from an initial introduction or networking conversation to setting up a sales conversation. In the next section we're going to cover what to do when someone contacts you. When you get an email or they call you and you've not spoken with them before. How do you handle that situation?

Toolbox

Checklist for Action: Pre-Sales Conversation Starter Questions

Use this action checklist to open up a pre-sales conversation with a potential client you've met at a networking event or other social event. The coach approach requires you to lead the conversation by asking questions. Make it conversationally appropriate to the context of where you happen to be. Design your own questions from your own genuine curiosity or use these as a starter set once you've established rapport and sufficient trust to go down this path.

1. What do you find to be the most difficult part about being a leader in your industry?
2. What's the hardest part for you about being a leader?
3. What are your goals and aspirations in your career?
4. What are key objectives in your organization you're accountable for advancing?
5. What are you trying to achieve this year in your work?
6. How are you doing with that goal so far?
7. What are your current challenges?
8. What are you experiencing in your organization?
9. What are some trends or common challenges you're seeing in your industry?
10. What are you struggling with in your role?
11. Do you or anyone you know ever struggle to [*fill in your specialty focus*] (For example, Do you or anyone you know ever struggle to navigate the politics in your organization? Do you or anyone you know ever struggle to motivate your employees?)
12. Would it be helpful to you to have a thought partner to help you sort through that?
13. Would it be helpful to have some brainstorming help on strategies or tactics for resolving that challenge?
14. Does it make sense for us to set up a meeting to discuss that further?
15. Would it make sense for us to get together to talk about solving that challenge?

CHAPTER 7

Making Sure the Client Is Right for Coaching

Ian: In the last chapter we talked about meeting new people and that in-between discussion in which you're trying to establish whether you can set up a sales conversation. In those cases you know who you're talking to and have a feel for whether they may be a good client for you. But sometimes someone may contact you and you won't know much, or anything, about them.

Suzi: Particularly online, if someone contacts you through LinkedIn or because of an article they've read, or they found you through your website or they are emailing you because someone recommended you, or they've just heard about you and they are cold-calling you. What do you do to determine if this is someone with whom it would make sense to have a sales conversation?

Initial Research

Ian: Usually I try to do two things in these situations. Ideally the first step is to do a bit of quick research. Go to LinkedIn or to their website and do a broad-brush qualification. I always check to see if they are in the right sector for me or the right type of organization, and if not, I rule them out. You will have your own qualifications, of course. When I do rule someone out, I still get back to them and potentially point them toward someone more suitable, but I already know that I don't need to spend a lot of time on the phone with them.

Sometimes no matter how detailed you are on your website about what you do, or how clear you are with people who might send you referrals, you end up being contacted by people who just aren't suitable for working with you. They're actually looking for a completely different type of coaching (or coaching is not even the right avenue for them, yet they've been referred to you). The confidence to pass on working with someone who isn't a great fit is very freeing, and builds value in your network when you refer to colleagues.

Qualifying Questions

Suzi: Assuming they do pass the initial qualification, then it's time for a conversation to learn more about what they're interested in or what they need help with. Often, if they've emailed me, I'll drop them an email back and ask a few simple questions before I speak to them. The email would probably say something like, "It sounds like it might be sensible for us to talk, can I just ask you a couple of quick questions first?" I usually ask them about what they are trying to achieve, why they think I would be the right person to work with, and why now is a good time for them to progress. I'm trying to understand whether this is something they're serious about or not. I ask the same questions over the phone if someone calls in and I happen to answer the phone.

Ian: I am really looking for three things:

- Is the thing they want help with an issue that I can deal with?
- Is there a solid reason why they're talking to me? For example, have I been personally recommended to them or do they think that I'm uniquely positioned to deal with this? (Or am I on a list of twenty people they're calling?)
- Can I see that they are genuinely motivated? I want to ensure this is not just a fishing expedition but they have a real motivation to do something right now.

If they pass all three criteria I'll schedule some time to speak with them. Usually what I do is I also give them a couple of questions to think about before our actual meeting to help them prepare for our discussion.

Suzi: I consider what they're looking to accomplish and whether coaching is the right intervention for it. If so, do they value the process of coaching? Will they commit to the process of coaching? Are they coachable? Those are some of the qualifications I'm looking at as well - in addition to everything you mentioned.

I'm also looking at whether they able to pay. Is this something that they have the backing of their organization to do, and is the procurement system all lined up and ready to go? Or are they deciding if they want to pay it themselves, or are they just starting the process and it will take months to figure out how to get it through the budget at their organization? You want to determine where their organization is in the decision making around this as well as how far into the research and procurement process they are. That really helps to decide whether (or when) it makes sense to go forward. Is this something that you're going to be investing a lot of time in to help their organization get up to speed or do they already purchase coaching services? Do they already have a system in place and the dollars approved? Are they able to move forward? Those are the kinds of things that you're going to try and get to in a qualification conversation, especially if it's someone coming to you whom you haven't targeted. Incoming referrals are exciting, but it's important to think clearly and protect your time, if they are not an ideal fit for you. Not all incoming referrals are actually potential business.

Ian: The next steps of having a sales conversation with them and following up are time consuming. Especially in a corporate where you may need to have multiple calls and they need to work their way through the decision network to get approval. So you don't want to start down that route unless you've got a good sense that this actually has a decent chance of going ahead.

Much of this depends on how busy you currently are. If you have a lot of leads, you can obviously afford to set tighter qualifications around who you will spend time speaking with. But if you have more time and fewer leads, you may be willing to go a bit further down the route of speaking to them face-to-face to do the qualification. But generally speaking, I think people underestimate how valuable their time is and they don't qualify enough.

Suzi: Now that we've looked at how we handle these initial discussions to spot an opportunity or to qualify someone who has contacted us, the next step is to set up the sales conversation itself.

Toolbox

Checklist for Action: Qualifying Questions for Inbound Inquiries

Use this action checklist to qualify potential clients so that you can determine if it makes sense for you to spend time in a sales conversation with them. Whether someone has found you through social media, or an email introduction, or another inbound inquiry, you'll want to figure out if this is someone to move into a sales conversation or not. First, consult LinkedIn to see if they are the type of organization or leader you wish to work with prior to calling them. Then you can proceed with these questions:

1. What are you looking for coaching to help you with?
2. What are you interested in accomplishing if we work together?
3. What type of coaching are you looking for?
4. What industry/ sector are you working in?
5. What are you trying to achieve?
6. Why is now a good time (the right time) for you to progress with coaching?
7. Why have you come to me at this time? What are you hoping I can do for you?
8. Where did you find me?
9. How motivated are you to do something about this right now?
10. Do you think what you're looking to accomplish is something that coaching is the right intervention for?
11. What other solutions have you tried already? Is coaching the best solution for this issue or challenge?
12. Do you value the process of coaching, and are you able to commit to the process of coaching?
13. Are you coachable?
14. Are you able to afford this solution?
15. Has your organization already approved the budget and procurement process for you to begin coaching?
16. How does your organization typically make coaching decisions?
17. What will it take for you to move forward on coaching from the organization's perspective?
18. Who else in your organization needs to be involved in this decision?
19. What next steps would make sense?

CHAPTER 8

Setting Up the Sales Conversation

I an: In this chapter we're going to look at the detailed process of setting an appointment with a potential client for a sales conversation.

Seizing the Moment in Person

Suzi: Okay, at this point you've met someone, either you found the person or he found you, you've had some initial conversation qualifying the intent and opportunity, and now you need to figure out how to get the sales conversation going. Basically, it's just the next conversation where you and the other person have actually said "yes" to moving forward together to whatever step is next. You've at least agreed it makes sense to get together and chat about whether or not to be working together. The real purpose behind a sales conversation is to help potential clients make a decision about what will serve them best. We must, however, avoid going too far - jumping into sales - when at a networking or social event or after a presentation. If you recall, we discussed the value in respecting the context of the event. Instead, you can set an appointment in that moment and preserve the sanctity of the context in which you're having the conversation. If you're able to skillfully set an appointment with that person, you can revisit the sales conversation when there's a boundary around that conversation and there's a safe time and place set aside to honor having that conversation. It makes it a sacred space to continue being social at the event as well as knowing that you've got earmarked an appointment for the sacred conversation of exploring what's next. In person, the quickest way to do that is to say, "Hey, do you happen to have your calendar on you? Let's take a quick look," and you can offer a specific date and time. Just one. Don't say, "Let's email about when we'll get together" because that takes your role of leadership out of it. You want to lead setting up that meeting, and if you can do it in that moment, all the better.

Ian: There is a far greater chance of getting it set up in that moment because you have that positive human connection going. Once you're out of the room, they'll get a bunch of emails and ten more appointments to be scheduled and the pressure of the working day, and all of a sudden they're less keen to commit to a meeting. It's not that they don't want to have that meeting with you, but other priorities take over. You want them to consult the calendar right then and pencil something in.

Suzi: Yes, because at that moment, they are present to either their pain that you can help solve or the opportunity to gain in working with you. You want to harness the excitement of the moment. With technology today, most people have their calendar on their smartphone or handheld device and you can take care of it on the spot. We suggest naming a specific time - "Let's set something up for next Wednesday at 3 o'clock" - as opposed to asking, "What looks good for you?" When you ask that question, they look through their calendar and are reminded of how busy they are. If you ask for a specific time, they will be less distracted by the other appointments they'd see if looking for an opening and instead they'd focus on that one date and time to see if they are, indeed, available.

Ian: You're just making it easy for them. Otherwise they have to do a bunch of mental juggling themselves to figure out when the best time is. Whereas if you suggest something, they just have to think - is this good, yes or no?

Suzi: Right, and then it also takes away the the internal discussion they might have with themselves of whether or not they really want to meet with you because instead of "Do you want to meet," it is "Do you want to meet Wednesday at 3?" - which is a very different approach. They start looking specifically at Wednesday at 3 to see if they *can* meet and they've already taken themselves out of the internal dialogue of *if* they want to meet.

Ian: You reach that point when you realize that they're interested in what you're talking about but now is not the right time and you need to have that follow up.

Suzi: Before I suggest a time, I usually say something like, "Would it make sense for us to get together to talk about that more?" Or some variation on that, like, "It sounds like it would make sense for us to set aside time to really dive into this, and it doesn't make sense for us to do that now because of where we are."

Ian: I use the exact same words quite often: Does it make sense? Would it make sense? I think it works well because it provides them with some wiggle room. You're not forcing something on them, and they're not accepting a meeting just to be polite. It should be easy for them to say it's not a good time for them.

You're also not overselling. You're not saying, "This could be brilliant and you'll get great benefits resulting from it and your organization will double in size and you'll become a great leader." It's too early for that.

Suzi: This is the coach approach to connecting with your prospective client. It's collaborating with them in an equal partnership like you would do in a coaching conversation, but you're doing that in the process of helping them move to whatever the next step in your sales or business development process is. In this case, the next step is to have a meeting specifically to discuss whether or not it makes sense to do work together. You can't assume. The coach approach really is the invitation for them to step into that dance with you and if it's not right, it's not right. It's being willing to honor that you don't know if it could work for them or not, and it's asking the question. It's bringing your coaching skills into play in this part of the process.

Setting an Appointment on the Phone

Suzi: The phrasing though is slightly different when you're in the face-to-face networking conversation versus over the phone. The language I would use on the phone or with leaving a voice-mail message is a little bit different because then you're just setting an appointment. Here's a simple three-step script for setting appointments.

The formula is 1) identification statement, 2) purpose of the call, and 3) request for the appointment. It should literally be just that fast.

The first piece of the script would be the **identification statement**. That's where you say who you are and how you got to them. If I were talking to you on the phone Ian, I might say, "Hi Ian, this is Suzi Pomerantz. Our good friend Jim Smith suggested that we should talk. He thought that it might make sense for us to talk about helping coaches get massive results by combining my Seal the Deal work and your marketing expertise." The second piece is **the purpose of the call**. You say, "I'm calling because Jim thought I might be able to help you with something. He told me he knew you're challenged by X... it might make sense for us to get together and talk about that." Then you **request the appointment**, as the third step. "Does it make sense for us to get together? If so, let's set up a call for Thursday at 5." Again, go with the specific date and time. You'll notice I didn't go into a whole long sales pitch about my twenty-plus years of experience or who I've served or what I helped them to do. I didn't do any of that. This is specifically just to set the appointment like you call to make a dental appointment. I would use a similar process in an email. If we've been connected by email, I might do that in a response email suggesting a time when we can get on the phone to talk to learn more about what we might do together.

Ian: At this point, if you talk too much you'll talk yourself out of a meeting rather than talk yourself into a meeting. You're not trying to sell them on buying your coaching services. You're just trying to set up a meeting with them and the justification for the meeting is encapsulated in your reason for calling. When you say, "Jim suggested I might be able to help you" or you mention that they may be looking for some support in a particular topic, then if that topic is important to them, it should be enough to justify participating in a short meeting or call with you. When you speak to them initially you're not trying to get them to hire you as a coach. All you're doing at this stage is trying to set an appointment for a meeting.

Suzi: Remember that you're setting a pure exploration meeting as the next step. There's no attachment on your end to getting the deal and there's no commitment on their end to agreeing to anything. So you're inviting them to an exploration, which is very safe for them. Sometimes you don't have the reasons for meeting because it's a referral (so and so said we should talk).

Ian: In that case, mentioning the person's name is often enough. If it's someone they trust and they know that person has recommended you, it's usually enough for them to be comfortable having a meeting with you.

Suzi: In that case, I might say, "Ian, you know our mutual friend Jim said that I should talk to you. I trust Jim, I'm not even sure *what* we should talk about, but let's get together. I'm confident that if Jim thinks it makes sense for us to talk that the two of us can figure out what those connection points are, so let's set up a call to explore. How's Tuesday at 11 a.m.?"

Ian: It could be that it ends up with a discussion not being about potential coaching at all but it could be a great networking contact for you for the future. The thing to bear in mind with every discussion you have is to be open to how you can help that other person and how they can help you. Every discussion is not necessarily going to end in a sales conversation. It could be, if you're open to other opportunities, that the person isn't right for you right now but could be a great person to introduce you to other people.

Toolbox!

Checklist for Action: Setting an Appointment for a Sales Conversation

Use this action checklist to set up an appointment for a next conversation to have a full sales conversation. Harness the excitement of the moment when the potential client is aware of the problem that they believe you can help them to solve.

1. Would it make sense for us to get together to talk about that more?
2. It sounds like it would make sense for us to set up another time to get into this further.
3. Do you happen to have your calendar on you? Let's quickly look at [*name a specific day, date, and time*] to explore this further.

CHAPTER 9

Getting Clients to Come to You Using Online Systems

Ian: The same principles we've talked about apply also to the online world. In the previous chapters, we've covered two of the most common situations that you're going to find yourself in when you want to transition to a sales conversation. That's when you're having a networking conversation and an opportunity pops up or when someone calls or emails you. But there are other, technology-based ways of initially finding clients, and with each of these you want to have appropriate transition to a sales conversation.

Suzi: We talked about many of the different ways that you can go about finding clients, but let's talk specifically about brainstorming lead-generating opportunities. There's the networking meeting and there's the referrals that we've just talked about, but there's a whole host of other ways that people could come to you and we call that lead generation. Those things you could set up, systems you could set in place to generate leads coming to you. Again, this goes not just to the networking side but really more on the marketing side: teleclasses that you might lead, webinars you might lead, newsletters you might send out, YouTube videos that you're creating, social media, and so forth. Ian's got some perspectives on how your website could be a really good lead-generating tool. What are some of the best approaches we can use there?

Ian: If you look at all these different methods of lead generation, the thing to bear in mind is that at the end of the day, all you want is a face-to-face or a telephone meeting with a well-qualified potential client, and sometimes that takes multiple steps. In the situations we've been talking about where you've met someone in person or you've been referred to someone or they've called you, then the appropriate next step is usually to go straight to setting up the meeting as long as you know enough about them and what they want.

In other cases where there's less personal interaction, you probably need more steps in the process. If you're looking at your website for example, there are typically two big reasons why people come to your site:

1. They may come to your website if they are actively looking for coaching help and support right now, and they are searching for a coach to help them. In such a case they'll probably fill in your contact form or give you a phone call. Then it turns into the situation that we talked about earlier where they contact you and you go through a process of qualifying them then setting up a meeting or call.

2. The more common situation is that someone visiting your website is in the earlier stages of their decision making. They have a problem or a challenge or a goal they want to address, and they're looking for useful information about it - perhaps to help them diagnose their problem better. Or perhaps they're looking for ideas on different solutions. They usually haven't yet decided that they need coaching.

   In this case, if you're using your website for lead generation, then what you need on your website is useful content about the problems and challenges that you help people with. This is what will help people to find you as they search. So as Suzi mentioned earlier, one topic coaches help client with is the internal politics tied up with being a leader. If that's what you help leaders and executives with, then articles about internal politics, the issues involved, and strategies you can use to address them will attract people to your site. So your articles cover what some of the issues are, simple strategies you can use to address them, and tips on how to make your new ideas stick. That way when people come to your site, they see those ideas, they see that you know what you're talking about, and that then leads them to examples of your work and testimonials. Then they might contact you directly or they might choose to sign up for your regular newsletter where you can pro-actively communicate with them.

   By signing up for your newsletter, they get regular updates from you about that particular topic, and over time your credibility builds further. As time passes, they may get more and more ready to hire a coach, so ideally when the time is right for them to hire someone, because they're receiving regular value from you about that particular topic, you should be the first person they reach out to.

In addition to just a plain email newsletter that goes out every month or every week that has a useful article in it about the topic that you coach on, you can be much more engaging and interactive in your emails. You can ask people questions. There's no reason why an email newsletter has to be just news or information. You can have a shorter one and you can write a short article about a particular issue, dealing with politics in an organization for example, and at the bottom of that article, you can have a question to them, "Are you seeing these sort of challenges in your organization?" Or "What's the number one challenge related to politics that you face in your organization?"

You're looking to begin a dialogue with potential clients who get your emails. A small percentage of the people who receive that newsletter for whom that issue is really pressing and urgent may well email back to you and say, "Actually the biggest issue for me is this..." Then you email to them and say, "Well, have you thought about this and this..." and you begin to get into a conversation with them, which leads to "Why don't we just pick up the phone and have a quick chat about this and maybe I can give you some ideas." Then it's exactly like the networking conversation we were talking about before. Then you're looking for all those signals and asking the same questions; in this way you move people from not knowing you to knowing there's a useful resource in your site to actually interacting with you as if it was a networking conversation.

That's the way I tend to use my website for lead generation. People find my site because they're coming for useful information. Then on the site they get offered a really useful free report or video in one of the top areas I coach in, and they sign up to get regular emails from me with tips and ideas. The newsletter doesn't just give them information, it asks them questions; I also do a survey at least once a year. Often the information I send out deliberately has a question at the end to get people interacting with me. So I'm starting potential clients off with a simple one-way email newsletter but using it to start a dialogue with the people most likely to value my services.

Suzi: All of these are just different starting points for how to get to the one goal, at this stage of the process, which is to get a meeting where you're going to talk specifically about whether or not it makes sense to work together. There are other starting points. If you're doing a presentation of some kind, a seminar, a webinar, a teleclass, or a public speaking engagement, how do you get them from the lead to a sales conversation? If someone comes up to you after an in-person presentation, or someone sticks around for the Q&A after a webinar or a teleclass, or someone contacts you by email after one of these speaking engagements, how do you then transition them into getting the meeting? What do you say?

Ian: I think the first thing is that you have to prompt that interaction. After a webinar, people don't typically email you and ask a question. In their minds the webinar is over. So what you need to do is to prompt them to contact you. Let's say at a webinar, you do Q&A at the end of the webinar and you answer everyone's questions as they ask them live on the webinar. But for specific questions you say to them, "Look, if you want to go into that in more detail, just drop me a quick email and we can have a conversation there and I can give you some more ideas." This transitions them from the webinar where people are asking questions as audience members to a one-to-one discussion.

Your goal at the end of a live presentation or a webinar or a seminar is to transition people to a one-to-one discussion. The word *transition* actually sounds a bit manipulative. But what you're really doing is giving them the opportunity to have that one-to-one discussion with you.

At the end of a live presentation, you can take questions and then you can say, "That's all the time we have for this presentation but I'm around here for the next thirty minutes if you have a more specific question and you want to talk over some of these issues in more detail." When they do come up to you afterwards to ask that more detailed question, make sure to flip it around and ask them about the context of the question.

If someone says, "Ian, you did an interesting presentation about lead generation techniques, what would you say is the number-one method of getting people to your website?" Rather than just answering it, I would say, "Good question, but you know, as ever with these things, it all depends. Can you tell me a little bit more about your situation and why you're interested in asking that question?" Then they might say, "Oh well, my problem is I have x, y, and z, etc., etc." When you know what their challenge and their problem is, you can provide your answer in context and be more helpful to them, which leads to saying, "It sounds like some of those ideas might be appropriate to help you. Would it make sense to sit down and grab coffee sometime and talk about these issues in more detail and explore whether working together might be appropriate for you?"

As you can see, the discussion moved into the exact networking conversation we were talking about before where you get into that discussion of whether it makes sense to sit down and talk. It's the exact same on the webinar as well. People will ask Q&A at the end, but for those who want more details, try to get them to email you afterwards and then you can answer that question while turning it around and asking them a question. In that way you begin to lead the conversation so that if it's appropriate they'll reveal to you what their particular challenge is and you can talk about whether it would be appropriate to sit down or get on the telephone or whatever your next step is.

Suzi: The coach approach here really is coming from the mindset of service, seeking to help, offering the invitation and coming from that place of genuine curiosity. It's not that anyone has to contact or come to you afterwards, but in your commitment to be of service, you are opening a door and making an offer and an invitation. Some people will walk through that and some people won't. Some of the people who walked through the door that you opened will be appropriate target market people for you and some of them won't. But there's still that genuine curiosity and exploring the opportunity and really helping them and you qualify whether or not it makes sense to move in to the next conversation. I've seen the rookie mistake some coaches make after speaking by diving into the sales conversation with one individual right then and there while a whole long line of people wait to talk to them. That doesn't help anybody, and it kind of goes back into honoring the space and the context of where you are. If you're at the end of the presentation and there's a whole long line of people waiting to talk to you, you want to very quickly determine if it make sense to have a separate conversation where you will explore if it makes sense to go to the next step. Then move on to the next person in line. The quicker you can do that, the better it serves everybody.

Ian: If there are ten people there and you've got half an hour, you've really only got three minutes each. If there's only person, you can spend a little bit more time with them. But even then when you've got more time, the setting usually isn't right. You can talk about it a bit further and do some more qualification, but you probably need a quieter and more intimate environment where you can have a more in-depth discussion. The environment in the bar after the presentation is probably not the best place in the world for that conversation.

Suzi: If you take nothing away other than this point, we want you to know that there is a progression between finding the prospective client, teeing them up as a lead, and actually securing the lead, which is what happens in a sales conversation. We want you to understand that there is a whole in-between step that many people either skip over or don't know to put in place.

It's a critical step with a lot of different starting points and possible avenues, but the ultimate goal is to take the coach approach to sharing an opportunity or an invitation with the person on the other side, inviting them into a conversation with you that has a specific purpose of exploring whether or not it makes sense for the two of you to work together. There's no need to rush this part of the process. You can savor this. Like the little *amuse bouche* in a fine restaurant that comes in between the appetizer and the main course. This is a lovely time because this is also what nurtures and secures the relationship even if ultimately you don't go forward and do business. This securing of the relationship during this stage of the process often generates huge referral leads for you later down the line, whether or not this person buys from you directly.

Ian: You want the experience that people have with you in these discussions to be overwhelmingly positive whether you end up having the sales conversation afterwards or not.

Suzi: Exactly.

Ian: Now in the next chapter we're going to move on to having sales conversations with potential clients.

Toolbox!

Checklist for Action: Sales Actions Kick-Starters

Use this action checklist to kick-start your sales activities if you don't know where to start or if you just want to get your sales results unstuck.

1. Determine your target market and make a target list.
2. Determine who you would like to approach with which offering and list them.
3. Determine potential referral stream sources and begin requesting referrals and leads.
4. Determine your call list to set up first appointments/meetings.
5. Start making calls, keeping the numbers game in mind.
6. Track your progress and move people through your sales process systematically.
7. Continually keep your pipeline filled so that you will not be attached to any one particular lead or prospect.
8. Explore direct and indirect means of keeping in contact with everyone in your process.
9. Keep making calls, keep setting up meetings.
10. Follow up, follow up, follow up.
11. Ask for the business!
12. Provide excellent customer service.

Toolbox

Marketing Communication Strategies

The Coach Approach of different ways to find and connect with potential clients requires setting systems in place to drive clients to you and generating leads through various marketing communication strategies such as teleclasses, webinars, newsletters, YouTube videos, social media, and of course, your website.

The main goal of all of these lead-generating vehicles is to generate a face to face or telephone meeting with a qualified potential client. Starting points are:

Website

- Useful content about common problems and challenges you help leaders and executives to resolve.
- Sign up for your newsletter.
- Build credibility over time.
- Deliver regular value.
- People find it when looking for useful information.

Email Newsletter

- Must go out regularly and consistently.
- Be engaging and interactive; ask questions, send surveys.
- Share valuable content about a particular challenge common to your ideal clients.
- Begin a conversation via email.
- Transition the conversation to a phone call.
- Move people from not knowing you to actually interacting with you - first on your website, then on email, then by telephone, and then explore whether it makes sense to meet.

Presentation/Webinar/Teleclass or other speaking engagement

- Prompt folks to ask you a question after the fact.
- Invite people to email you for more ideas.

- Transition from their quick questions in the public forum to going deeper into their specific problem or goal in a 1:1 conversation; give them the opportunity.
- Flip it around and ask them for context of their question
- "Good question, can you tell me a little bit more about your situation and why you're asking that question?"
- When you know their challenge/ problem, you can answer in context, which is more helpful to them, and it also allows you to invite them to discuss it with you further offline.
- "Would it make sense to sit down and talk about that more?"
- Coming from a mindset of service, seeking to help, offering an invitation, and coming from a place of genuine curiosity.
- Explore the opportunity.
- Avoid actually having the sales conversation at the tail end of a presentation...especially when there's a line of folks waiting to talk to you!
- Connect quickly and, if appropriate, invite further conversation offline where timing and environment are right for that conversation.

CHAPTER 10

The Coach Approach to Helping Potential Clients Decide

Suzi: Successful sales conversations are all about helping clients make a decision. This happens in a conversation just like the coaching conversations, and it's critical to set the expectations for this conversation so that it's not perceived as a free coaching session by you or the potential client. Rather, it's a strategy session or an initial discussion about what you and your potential client might achieve together through coaching.

We're going to look at how to use this conversation with your potential client to help them determine what's right for them in terms of next steps with or without you. You are really helping them reach a decision and clarify if they want to be a client and are ready for that, if they're a match for you and you for them, and if you truly understand their issue and can help them solve it. It's different from a coaching conversation in that the agenda is the client's agenda in a real coaching conversation. However, in a sales conversation, you also have an agenda and you are the one who needs to be in the leadership role to balance the two agendas.

Your agenda is not just to get the client or get the business, because that can have a tinge of desperation and is likely to repel a potential client. Your goal is to make the right decision for both of you. You want to be an equal in the conversation and not just be in service to the client's needs without attention to your own. When you're in service in a coaching conversation, you don't have an agenda. Your agenda disappears. You disappear other than being in service to the client and their agenda. That's what's different in a sales conversation. In a sales conversation you're also serving your own agenda, which is to help them decide what's best for them while also balancing helping yourself decide what's best for you.

Now because your potential client will have less experience of coaching than you, it's really up to you to gently lead them through the process. You can't just sit back and allow them to lead because they don't really know where they're going. You have to lead the process, but make sure they're comfortable with how it's going.

This is also about managing yourself, because as coaches, we love to help. We love to make a difference. We love to get in there and coach, so we have to hold ourselves back and pull up the reins of the conversation so that we don't dive headlong into a coaching conversation too soon, because that will derail the sales conversation.

Let's take an in-depth look at the sales conversation now. We provide a modular approach to that conversation rather than a step-by-step guide because you'll need to use your listening skills and your inquiry skills to read the signals from your potential clients. By listening well, you'll know which puzzle piece of the conversation to put in. You'll also recognize when the person you're talking to can't make the decision by themselves and you need to involve others (for example, more senior executives for approval or other functions). We're going to identify all the different modules and puzzle pieces you could use, depending on the signals from your client.

Getting to No Quickly

Ian: We previously discussed the idea that no is a gift. Keep that in mind throughout your entire sales conversation. When you begin to feel it is not the right time to proceed or they're not necessarily thinking you're the right person to go ahead with, or they're not just clear at all on what it is they're trying to achieve or whether it's worth getting there. Often the temptation at that stage can be to plow ahead and try to sell to them anyway. You might think, "I'll bring them on board as a client and we'll sort it all out afterwards." Usually that's not the right approach.

Suzi: If there's a no waiting in the wings, you want to force it on stage early on. That means you want to find out sooner than later that it's a no so that you don't waste your time and theirs. Also the more quickly you get clarity, you can shift the conversation to something else that perhaps the two of you might do together, and you stop pursuing the sales angle.

One way to be comfortable with no is to remember that it can be in your best interest and theirs to have them decide not to work with you. What's the coach approach to helping your potential clients decide *not* to work with you? It could be that instead you make a referral, which would help a colleague of yours as well as help them. It could be that coaching is not the right intervention in which case you can help them identify what intervention might be better suited to their situation. You do this from a helping frame of mind.

Check your mindset: You never want to come at it from the perspective of wanting to persuade or convince them of anything. Your job is to help them through making the decision that is right for them. Some basic questions help with that determination: Is this the right problem for them to be working on? Is it important enough for them to do something about it now? Is coaching the right intervention for this problem? Are you the right coach for the problem? Approach each of those questions from a completely objective place; you're setting aside your agenda of needing or wanting the business. Look at it from your perspective of how you can be of service to this potential client and help them to decide if it's not going to work. Get that out of the way first.

Ian: Of course it is also legitimate for you to say no. The client might want to work with you, but they may not be a great fit for you. Your personalities may not click, or they may be looking for a different coaching style than you prefer to work in. Maybe the problem they have isn't something you cover with your coaching. Or you may see that what they really need is training or some other intervention rather than coaching.

As you go through the discussion, it's up to you to raise the issues you're seeing. You might reflect back to the potential client some of the things you're hearing from them. Or if it's from your side, share what you're concerned about.

Suzi: Sometimes you've connected with the potential client and discovered now is not the right time. There's a timing issue. That raises the issue about what you're going to do between now and sometime later when it might be the right time. This is the gray area of no. I am talking about a genuine "not now" and not a smoke screen. An example of a genuine "not now" would be when it is not the right timing in the organization's fiscal year.

Ian: To determine if it's a "not now" that actually means no, I phrase the follow up in a way to get them to admit that their "not now" means "actually, not ever." For example, if they say, "Oh we just don't quite have the budget yet," then I might say, "Okay, why don't we agree the next step that when you do have the budget, we'll get back together. So let's arrange a meeting right now for a time when you do have the budget." If it was a genuine "we don't have the budget but I'm ready to go ahead," then they would be perfectly happy to meet when the budget is ready. In that case they might say, "Okay the budget is going to be ready on December 3, so let's set a meeting on December 7." On the other hand, if they're unwilling to set a date then it's a strong signal that their "not now" really means "no." Being specific and setting dates cuts through that smoke screen.

Remember that it's always best to get the real issue out on the table. An effective question to make that happen is this: "Look, it sounds like actually you're not that comfortable yet in going ahead, am I right?" Bring the no to center stage, as Suzi says.

Suzi: There's no need to shy away from asking a very direct question. I will sometimes say, "Not now or not ever?" Or I might say, "Are you just being polite because you don't want to say no, or is there really a later time that this makes sense?"

Ian: If the "not now" is genuine, then set up something definite. The time frame between your current conversation and the next date on the books determines whether you follow up and nurture the relationship. If it's just a few weeks, then you can let it go. But if it is a long way into the future, then get permission to keep in touch in between.

Bear in mind that keeping in touch does not mean nagging. You don't want to chase or repeatedly ask whether they're ready. Keeping in touch is simply communicating with them on a regular basis in a way that continues to build your relationship with them.

Suzi: Let's say you get in touch with them once a month between now and whenever you're supposed to connect again. You don't need to call once a month and say, "Hey, are we still good? Is everything still moving forward?" A better option might be to email a relevant article to them and say, "Hey, I saw this and I was thinking about you and our conversation and I'm looking forward to our next steps." Or it might be a quick call to ask how their vacation was. You're just nurturing the relationship. Put it on the calendar and reach out in one way or another.

Ian: You have to recognize that during this in-between time, they would have seen hundreds and hundreds of other emails and met dozens of other people so you've got to do something to stay on their mind. One thing that helps is debriefing yourself after the meeting with them. Write down all the topics that could be interesting and valuable to them based on your discussion, including both business and non-business topics. In a month's time you're not going to remember all the details of what you discussed in the meeting if you don't write it down. But when you've captured those details you have a great "database" of ideas to follow up with. You could send them a relevant article (ideally one you've written yourself, but anything useful is a positive step). Or see whether there are events you can invite them to or people you can introduce them to. You want to add value and be useful so that when you get back to meeting with them, your relationship will have strengthened rather than decayed.

Suzi: Now that we've covered the "not now" side of no, let's look at other cues that a no is waiting in the wings. Energy level is an important flag. Depending on the person you're talking to and the context of what your coaching focuses on, you use different words. With a chief exec or CFO it might be about the financial benefit: "What would the bottom line impact of that be?" With other people it might be more like this: "What would the personal benefit of that be for you?" But as they are asking questions and trying to draw them out, note whether they're really struggling to come up with anything or if you detect that the energy level isn't there. That's a key signal of the "no waiting in the wings."

The "Unsell"

Ian: Sometimes when I'm opening up a conversation with a client, I just ask a gentle question like, "So tell me a little bit about why you're addressing this right now?" If they don't have a great answer to this, or they say, "My boss told me to," then that's a warning sign. They should really be getting excited as they talk about what they might get from it and they should be able to clearly elaborate some of the benefits they anticipate from it. Of course, you want to help them see the wider benefits too if they don't immediately grasp them. If they say they anticipate a feeling of personal satisfaction as a result of changes made due to your coaching, you might say, "Well and what impact do you think that might have on your career?" If possible, help them to see that the true benefit is much greater than what they currently see. Of course you can't force it on them. They may say, "No, no, there's nothing in it for my career." If you get that feeling from them, then do exactly what we've said and put it on the table. Say, "Look I'm getting the feeling that this actually isn't such a big deal for you."

Suzi: In a situation like that you can gently explore: "Well, it sounds like you've kind of got this thing handled, so maybe this is not the most important thing. If not, what is?" Then you can go back to an exploratory conversation and say, "What's keeping you up at night? If this thing is important to your boss and you've already got it handled and you've already got the strategy in place for that, what's left? What's the next thing that's nagging at the back of your brain?" If they were to say, "Well, I don't know. There's nothing." Then that's you eliciting the no, bringing it out onto the stage. But if there *is* something else, then you're helping them decide if coaching is the right thing for that problem now that they're bringing up. Sometimes there are multiple layers of the conversation. But again the segments of that we are looking at are: **Is it the right problem, is it important enough, is the timing right, is coaching the right intervention, and are you the right coach?** You want to look at all five of those elements and sometimes you have to do different rounds of explorations around each one of those elements.

Ian: During that process, by highlighting that it seems like the issue is being covered elsewhere or that it's under control already or that you're not sure this is the right thing to be focusing on coaching, you are actually earning a good bit of credibility. Because you're not jumping in and trying to sell them and instead you're clearly trying to make sure that you're doing the right thing for them, you'll find that they're more likely to open up and tell you what the real issue is or tell you there isn't one. That's especially important if they haven't approached you for help directly themselves, for example if someone has referred them or you've approached them. In those cases there's a higher chance that they're just being polite and there's not really an immediate opportunity to work together so it's best to force that out into the open.

Suzi: It's true that your credibility and their regard and respect for you increases when you almost talk them out of buying from you. I call that approach "the unsell" - it's you collaboratively helping them to decide if it's not the right problem or not the right timing or not important enough to handle now. If they seem uncertain, you can actually force the no by saying something like, "Well, you know we could work together but I don't think it makes sense. This doesn't seem to be the best use of your money to work with me. I think there are other ways you could get this handled." Then suggest to them what might help - a training session, a webinar, or whatever it might be. Talking them into why they don't need you or why they don't need any kind of expensive intervention really helps them value you more as someone who is going to be honest and trustworthy, who has their best interest in mind, and who will tell it to them straight. I'm not advocating that use this as a gimmick just to try to build credibility. It's something to use if you genuinely believe it's the right thing to do and the increased credibility is a side effect.

It's also helpful for you as the coach to not be so hooked into the need to get the business that you're not willing to walk away from it. Being willing to unsell them and force the no will work often work to your advantage because it leads them to realize they really do want to work with you.

Ian: You benefit from not wasting time chasing something that's going to turn into a no anyway. And it benefits you because you get increased respect and often that will come to pay you back later because they'll recommend you to others. Whether it does pay you back or not, it's the right thing to do.

Suzi: I often think about it like a dating process metaphor where so many people are going into the sales conversation hoping to get marriage proposal, but really you've got to date for a while before you're ready to commit to a long-term relationship. Sometimes it's better to find out in the first date that you're not a match and it does not make sense to go forward together. Sometimes you don't know that until later in the process. But it's always useful to figure out if it's not going to work before you get into the long-term commitment.

Moving the Decision Forward

Ian: Even if it's not a no, it's not always as simple as a yes. There are other processes to be addressed. The purpose of this chapter is to show you what those other processes are and how to work with your client so that you go through that them successfully.

Suzi: This won't be part of every sales process but it's something to pay attention to because it may be necessary in certain organizations or in certain contexts. Often the client is not aware of the steps required to move forward within their own organization, so help them figure out the required steps.

Ian: Usually the bigger and the more complex the organization, then the more steps and hoops there are going to be (unless you're working with the person at the very top). Of course often in the public sector there are lots of official processes you have to go through.

We discussed earlier the different people involved in buying executive coaching services. There is the executive themselves but sometimes you'll need to involve one of the executive's bosses; a chief executive or a CFO or procurement officer may need to be involved to approve the decision. Sometimes HR needs to be involved. HR may have standards or qualifications for coaches, or maybe even a recommended short-list of coaches that you have to get on. The first step is figuring out with your client whether that's the case.

Suzi: Sometimes people are not aware of what's going on in their own organization. A segment of the organization may have a process or a procedure in place or even some preferred vendors for the coaching that they do in that organization, and you may not be part of that preferred vendor list. Part of what you want to do is help your client (and yourself) understand how their organization works. If a preferred vendor list exists, do you need to be on it or are they still allowed to work with you? This helps you but it also helps them figure out what conversations they need to have with whom to determine how to go about getting support for themselves in the organization. Sometimes organizations require a proposal, but that's an issue we'll address in a bit. Sometimes it's about escalating the connections that you have in that organization - going both broader and deeper in the organization. This is often necessary when you're dealing with an executive, because the challenge that's presenting involves a lot of people and you have to get deeper and broader in the organization to maybe do interviews or to get a better handle on the context or the culture.

Ian: That's even necessary in order for you to do the coaching you need to do.

Suzi: It may also be necessary to helping your client be able to make the decision to move forward. They need to know what they need from other key stakeholders and understand the decision-making process not only in their organization, but in their mind. If you're dealing with a very senior level executive, you want to understand their decision making, internal decision tree, and thinking-analysis process as well as the organization's decision and procurement process.

Ian: Sometimes even when there is not an official need to go and check things with other people, they still want to do so. They may have an informal mentor in the organization and they would like their opinion. Sometimes, too, bringing in a coach may raise a public perception issue that the executive may worry about. They may want to speak to some of their colleagues about it first. Even though they may well have the complete authority to make this decision alone, they may want to confer with others before doing so.

The Ask

Suzi: Sometimes what's needed in order to move the decision forward relies on you - you need to do the "ask". Even though this conversation is about helping your clients find what's needed, really we're in a sales conversation. If the "sales" word trips you up - feels aggressive or pushy or manipulative or conniving - you may need to reframe your mindset. You can have all the great conversations in the world, but at some point you have to develop a muscle and comfort around asking for the business.

Ian: It's like the dating metaphor again. After dating for some period of time, if you want to get married, someone is going to have to pop the question. It could be either of you, but as a coach, you want to be proactive enough to do the asking rather than waiting forever for your potential client to do it. In the world of client and coach, if you wait for the client seal the deal, then you're the person who will be suffering at the end of the day, wishing for more in the relationship.

Suzi: Trouble often comes when a coach hasn't maintained the boundaries of the sales conversation and has jumped into the coaching conversation prematurely. Then they find themselves in a predicament similar to couples who just keep dating and dating, neither one puts an end to it or makes a stronger commitment. Essentially what happens in these situations is that you set up a next conversation thinking you're advancing the sales conversation, but if you've slipped into coaching, you're really setting up another coaching conversation. Over time, the client gets some free coaching and there's never an "ask" - meaning you as the coach never ask them to become your paying client. There's no commitment to get into a coaching agreement or spell out the steps of the contract or anything like that. That's just something to be wary of and to be honest with yourself if you're doing that. There are appropriate boundaries to set around the sales conversations that are distinct and separate from coaching conversations, and those enable you to establish the essential mindsets and boundaries that will allow you to be paid for coaching as opposed to coaching for free.

Permission to Discuss Process Issues

Ian: It's worth being aware that this question might come up at different times in the sales conversation or process. If you get a feeling that they will have to ask permission, it usually is a good idea to bring this topic up quite early on. You're going to be a waste of time for both of you if it's going to be a "no" for process reasons or you spend ages planning out what you're going to do together only to find there's no budget or you're not on the list of three coaches they're allowed to use.

Ian: Early on in the sales conversation after you've established rapport, you want to get permission to discuss all of the process issues with a question like this: "Do you mind if I just ask you a couple of questions about how your organization typically handles things like hiring a coach?" They're not going to say no to that. They might not know the answers, which is important, because in that case you make plans together to go and find the answers. It's important to uncover the issues earlier rather than later.

Suzi: During the discussion you want to listen for the ways the two of you can collaborate to move the decision forward. What do they need to help them make a decision, and what does the organization need to move forward? You're really exploring with the client. What does forward look like? Is forward a next step or is forward a decision? If it's a decision, what's involved in the decision and who's involved in the decision? What is the timeline on the client's side? What do they need from you? Part of what you're doing is acting as a guide and a leader for your client in that conversation. It's a specific part of the conversation that could happen at any time in the sales conversation, but it's yours to lead. It's not theirs to lead even though sometimes they'll throw bits of information out about it. For instance, sometimes they'll say of their own accord, "Well great, I'm ready to move forward, but I've just got to get the buy-in from the CEO."

Ian: That's a signal.

Suzi: But if they don't offer it, we as the coaches have to lead that part of the conversation because it's important to find out who the stakeholders are, what the decision-making process is, what else is needed in order to move forward on the decision.

Ian: Once you reach the stage where you sense that they are happy to move ahead, it's time to ask, "What do we need to do to make this happen?" Or you can say, "Typically in your organization, who else gets involved in these sort of decisions? Who are the stakeholders?" You can come up with your own phrasing, but you need to ask about who will be involved and the stages that are involved.

The "P" Word

Suzi: If they come back to you and say the word *proposal,* as in "We need a proposal from you," then there's another line of questioning for you to pursue. Sometimes, they really *do* need a proposal. Sometimes, they say they need a proposal because they don't want to say no - they feel badly because they've invested a lot of time in a conversation with you. This is just another opportunity for you to investigate whether that's a smoke screen for a potential no or whether they're trying to put it off for a different time or whether they need one in order to move forward because they have to show something in writing to internal stakeholders (or the board) to get the funding.

I usually handle a request for a proposal like this: "I would be happy to do that. What I have found is that if we work together on the key components required for the proposal to be most relevant, it makes it more effective for whoever it is that you need to submit the proposal to." This is a great way to uncover who the decision maker really is. That's where I start. The client might then tell you that the proposal needs to go to the CEO and the board. Then you can lead them with: "So let's just talk for a minute about what they would need to see in order to move forward on it. What do you think the proposal should include? What matters most to them?" Oftentimes if they have a whiteboard or a flip chart in their office, we'll just get up right then and there and put the bullet points on the board together. In other words, you co-create the proposal with your potential clients so they're engaged and invested in it, and then you say, "You know what we might consider doing? We might consider delivering this in a meeting. So should we set up a meeting with your boss or someone from the board?" Or "Is there a time when it would be appropriate for us to present this to the board (or whoever the decision-maker might be)?" Ideally, you want to move the proposal forward with a meeting. You want to avoid putting hours into writing a document that you email back - and then it disappears into a black hole.

Ian: That's probably the biggest time waster that I know of. I've heard so many people say, "Oh, I submitted this proposal and nothing happened." The word *submit* often indicates you're doing it wrong. If you're working on the proposal together on a whiteboard, as Suzi suggested, and you run out of time in that meeting, don't say that you'll finish up the proposal and then submit it. Better to say that you'll finish drafting it and then you'll jointly finalize it to confirm it addresses everything.

If they're not willing to commit to working together on the proposal either in the meeting then and there or in a follow-up meeting or call, then it's highly unlikely that they'll ever commit to buying and working with you. If they really wanted to do this, they'd be willing to commit some of their time.

Suzi: Ideally, I like to get around the proposal altogether and say, "Well, what I much rather do is send you a letter of agreement. Let's make sure we're clear and aligned on what our agreement might be and instead of submitting a proposal, I'll submit to you a letter of agreement with details once we're on the same page so we can move forward sooner."

Ian: Often they don't need a proposal at all. It's almost just like an automatic reaction to ask for a proposal - whenever you need something, you ask for proposal. Very often a letter of agreement will work just as well. There are various legal and contractual things about proposals, letters of agreements, actual contracts, and so forth, but it's rare that a client really needs a formal proposal loaded with information. Whenever you're asked for a proposal, you should ask whether it's really needed and suggest something simpler.

Suzi: One, I submit a one-page letter of agreement saying: Here's what we talked about, here's what we think it would look like, and here's what the pricing would be. I'd much prefer to do that than a forty-page proposal that ends up in the circular file or junk folder.

Keep in mind that when you hear the word *proposal*, that does not mean you've sealed the deal. That does not mean you've closed the business. It could be smoke screen, it could be a "no," it could be a delay or it could actually be that they are not clear about the value, or it could be that in their procurement process they actually do need something called a proposal in writing from you. You've just got to do more digging. Don't take the temptation to think you've won and then run off to start working on a proposal until you're sure of its purpose and that there is an actual need for it. Don't assume there is a real need for a proposal at all without exploring further.

Ian: I think that's a vital point because the proposal itself is not a sales document. If they're not already convinced before you send them the proposal, then what you write in the proposal will almost never convince them. Whether it's a simple one-page letter of agreement or a detailed proposal, it should just be confirming what you've already agreed with them. There shouldn't be any new information in the proposal.

I often see coaches submit a proposal with new information they haven't already discussed with the client because they're almost frightened to talk about the price and the commercial elements of the deal. They don't talk about it and the first time the client sees it is in the proposal. Revealing the pricing for the first time in black-and-white on paper is not the way to do it. It should be discussed face-to-face. A proposal shouldn't be used an excuse to not talk about the tough things. You really need to get everything out first and then the proposal just confirms the agreement you've reached.

If a proposal has to be submitted to others for their buy-in, then you and your potential client should take the proposal together in-person to anyone who needs to approve it. That way you can explain all the key points. Sometimes clients are a bit wary when it comes to submitting things to their boss or the senior people, and they may be a bit wary that you might be trying to go behind their back and then persuade their bosses of something. Obviously it's in their best interest to be working with you to get this project, this piece of coaching to go ahead. But clients are often somewhat suspicious about outsiders trying to get to their boss, so using the "us" word makes it clear it's not about you going to see the boss behind their back with a proposal, we're in this together. Saying "us", "why don't we do this", not "I", "why don't I do this" works really well. It's "us" doing it together because the whole purpose of this is to help you achieve your goals. That's what I'm here for, to work with you to help you achieve your goals.

Suzi: It frames your role as being in support of them. You can frame it like this: "What support do you need in getting this through the system in your organization? If we go together to the board, does that support you? If we go together to your boss, does that support you? If we write this document together, does that support you?"

Ian: That kind of wording gets the point across subconsciously that you're on their side because everything you're suggesting is in their interest - helping them to achieve what they're trying to achieve.

Suzi: That ties up the discussion of helping your potential clients decide what's needed to move the decision forward. Keep in mind that this is kind of a modular approach because the sales process is dynamic. Next we're going to get into the value proposition and the actual sales conversation.

Toolbox

Questions to Surface the No

There's no need to persuade or convince them of anything. Help them make the right decision by asking these questions:

1. Is this the right problem, challenge, or issue to be working on?
2. Is this important enough to address now?
3. Is coaching the right solution?
4. Am I the right coach for this problem?
5. What will be the impact if you don't solve this problem now?

Ask yourself these questions to assess fit:

1. Am I the right coach for this client?
2. Is this client someone I can help, or is there any reason I wouldn't want to work with him or her?
3. Am I the right coach for this organization?
4. Are they the right client for me?
5. Is this the right problem for me?
6. Is this the right type of intervention for me to lead?

Strategies for Nurturing the Relationship until the Timing Is Right

When the answer is "not now," it's important to nurture the relationship and continue to engage with the client. Below are strategies for follow-up:

1. Set a meeting now for the future date when you know the budget will be available.
2. Map out with the client what needs to be done between now and then to advance anything that can be advanced.
3. Touch base once a quarter to see if anything has changed.
4. Set up something definite for a check-in down the road. Schedule a call or meeting.
5. Get permission to keep in touch between now and then, without nagging. Do something each time to continue to build the relationship - send an article, share relevant information, or call to check in about something other than "Are you ready yet?"
6. Take the lead to maintain and nurture the connection along the way.
7. Help them keep you at the top of their mind in a positive sense.
8. Write down all the topics that are interesting and of value to them so you have a tickler list to use for future touch-points.
9. Think about who you can introduce them to.
10. Are there events you can invite them to?
11. How can you elevate the level of your relationship with them between the first meeting and the future point when they are ready to act?

Value Proposition Prioritization Map

Use the chart below to evaluate whether you've hit all the key elements needed to help the client determine if it makes sense for them to move forward with hiring you to provide executive coaching services.

Decision Maker Name & Title	The Issue, Problem, Challenge or Need	Is it the Right Problem?	Is it Big and Important enough to work on?	Is Coaching the Right Solution for this Problem?	Is the Timing Right?	Am I the Right Coach?

Key Questions in the Buying Process

One of your key roles in the sales process is to help your client become clear about their own buying process so that you can help them determine how best to move the decision forward. The questions below will help you and your client navigate the buying process in their organization.

1. Who else needs to be involved in the decision?
2. Where is the funding coming from?
3. What's the proposal process?
4. What's the procurement process?
6. Is a formal proposal or presentation required?
7. Are there any pre-established criteria for hiring coaches?
8. Is there an approved vendor list?
9. If there is an approved vendor list, are you still allowed to work with me if I'm not on it?
10. What else do we need to know to understand your organization's formal criteria?
11. What else matters in the executive's personal decision making?
12. What buy-in is needed from other key stakeholders?
13. What do we need to move this decision forward?

Proposals and Letters of Agreement

Co-create the **proposal** with your potential client. Support them using the language of "we" and "us" in collaboration to help them move the decision forward in their organization. If they ask for a proposal, you can respond this way: "I'd be happy to provide a proposal, and if we work together it will be more effective for the people we will need to submit it to."

Then sort out with your client the following:

1. Who is the proposal for?
2. What do you think they will need to see?
3. What should the proposal include?
4. Should we present this to the board?
5. Is there anyone specific we should plan to present it to?
6. When should we present this to the other decision-makers?

If you and your client have already agreed about next steps, a proposal may not be needed, so you can say instead, "Rather than delay us with a proposal process, would it make sense to simply send you a **letter of agreement** so we can move forward?"

Include the following elements in your letter of agreement:

- Simple, one-page summary of what you've agreed
- Objectives of your work together
- Milestones or measures of success
- How you'll work together: logistics, time frames
- Any other stakeholders involved
- Pricing

CHAPTER 11

Working with You

Suzi: We have looked at the coach approach to help potential clients decide what's needed to move the decision forward, and, we have also looked at getting them to no quickly so that you can get clarity and move on. Then we looked at what it takes to move the decision forward in their organization. In this chapter, we're going to narrow in on the coach approach to helping potential clients decide to start working with you and there are two pieces of yes and no that we're looking for.

The Value Proposition

In this particular section, we're going to look at leading them through a coaching process for helping them gain clarity around their decision process and timelines. Here are the considerations:

- Do they know what their problem is and how big a problem it is and what the impact of that problem is?
- How important is it to them and their career as well as to their organization?
- Can we help them solve that problem and what's the risk to them or their organization if it remains unsolved?

We're going to assign value amounts to those specific areas and we call that series of questions **the value proposition**.

This is an opportunity to look at two different "yeses." You're helping them with a coaching process: this is a coaching conversation within a bigger sales conversation.

The coaching conversation is helping them with decision-making clarity around the problem and what they want to do to solve that problem, including whether it's the right problem and has the right amount of impact and importance. That adds up to the first yes. The second yes that we want to help them get to is whether you're the right person to help them solve that problem. So there are two yeses that we're playing with in this segment about how you and your coaching process can help your potential client mentally get to yes in both of those domains.

Ian: A key thing to bear in mind is that every client situation is different. As we've said before, this is not a static, linear process where you ask the same questions to them every time. When you're sitting down with a potential client for this meeting and you're discussing this, their mindset is going to be in a different place depending on their history. They may already have decided they wanted to move ahead and they're just talking to you about whether you're the right person. Or they know the area is a problem, but they're not sure whether it's worth solving yet. Or they may know they've got an issue but they're not quite sure exactly what to do or what the real problem is. You'll have to funnel down from your initial conversation to helping them get to, as Suzi said: Is this the right problem? Is it big enough that I want to address it? Do I want to address it? Do I want to work on it with you?

Suzi: This is one of those things that you are listening for and looking for at several stages of the sales process. This particular conversation could happen within a sales meeting, it could happen earlier on when you first received the referral, or it could happen in the midst of the networking conversation. The reason we're covering it here is for you to pay attention to looking for and listening for when this conversation is missing in your ability to move clients to the next step. What you're looking for and listening for is whether your potential client has their own mental clarity and energy around these two yeses (whether they want to solve the problem and if coaching is the solution to that problem). If you don't hear clarity and a yes, or, as we said before in the previous sections, if you don't hear a clear no, then that's the work for you to do in this conversation as the coach. To get in and have a nano-coaching conversation with them to help them get clear in either direction: yes or no to the problem, the solution, and you as part of the solution.

Ian: You have to do it in this order as well. Many coaches often jump to the second yes too quickly when the client hasn't really made the first yes yet. The client may be talking about the problem they have, and the coach immediately thinks that because the client has said they have a problem that they're ready to move forward and address it.

But just because the client has said they have a problem doesn't mean they're ready to move forward yet. It's a bit like the way that saying your knee hurts doesn't necessarily mean you want to have a surgery. It just means that it hurts. It's not the same as making a decision that you want to get that problem solved. If you jump immediately to talking about the next steps before they've mentally made the decision that they want to do something about it, then it will feel as if you are pushing them too far, too fast. This can cause a total disintegration of the sales conversation. Before you try to talk to the client about working with you, first determine if they've decided whether to do anything at all about their situation.

Suzi: In many ways, the value proposition conversation is a coaching conversation - to a point. You can begin the value proposition conversation with "What is the greatest challenge that you're facing right now?" or "What do you see to be the biggest challenge coming down the pike?" or "What are you hoping that coaching could help you solve?" or "What is it that you thought would make sense for us to talk about today in this conversation?" If you already know, then by all means, dive right in like you would in a coaching conversation and start pulling apart the problem. Start asking the questions that flesh out more of your understanding of the problems and all its tentacles in the organization and the way all of that that impacts the individual and their career as well as all the other important stakeholders in the organization. Consider all the places that the problem touches.

This is about looking at the system that the problem exists in and helping your potential client get clear about the problem, its branches and thorns, its impact, and the damage or delay or cost it is creating. You want to stay in the pain of the problem with them, and you do that with a lot of digging and questions, to help your client see and feel the pain and the breadth of it - the number of people it impacts. You want to keep opening and revealing and un-layering and asking questions like you would in the coaching conversation to really get to the core of the problem. How deep, how broad it is, how big it is, what does it look like, how does it show up? Anything that you would ask to get to all of the different flavors of the problem, all of the different places that it touches and impacts and then asking questions staying in the pain of the issue, keeping your client in the pain of it. Helping them paint a three dimensional picture of the pain that they or their organization is facing and keep asking those clarifying questions like - who does this touch and what is the impact of that touch and how many people are involved and what happens if you don't get that solved? Then asking them about the financial impact.

I will often ask them: "How much is this costing your organization? If you were to put a dollar amount, I know you might have to guess but if you have to guess or come up with a range, what is this costing your organization?" Pause and let them think about that. Really let them ponder, "What is this costing us?" Silence is your friend in this part of the conversation. You actually want your client to feel the discomfort. The number then will be much more real to them. If they don't say a big enough number, help them flesh out more of the places where you see it might be having a cost impact and then ask them also the flip side question: "What would it be worth, dollar-wise, to solve this? What would happen in your organization if you solve this? What would that mean in terms of cost savings or increased revenues or retention numbers?" You want a hard metric ($ or %) that the CEO or the senior executive can get their teeth around.

Ian: It's interesting that those two questions are not the same. They sound as if they're just the reverse of each other. What's the size of the problem versus what would you get if you solved it. But often you get different answers. For instance, suppose the problem relates to time wasted by the senior team because they're forever arguing in meetings. That's the original size of the problem. But when you say, "Okay, let's say that through coaching we'll be able to get your team all headed in the same direction and working together, what would that do for you? What would that be worth?" Often that trigger a different pattern of thinking and they realize there are many other areas of benefit. For example, it means they'll have more strategic alignment and they would all be working together. Once a client starts to talk through the broader impact, they'll get quite excited about it. When you're exploring with a client the size, scale, and impact of the problem, you want them to be energized by the discussion when it reaches its close and not depressed by it. People don't make decisions to move forward when they're depressed.

By bringing them out of the other side of the problem tunnel and talking through the size, scale, and impact (both financial and organizational), they begin to be excited about the solution rather than depressed about the problem. Of course, it does not have to be a problem. It could be an aspirational goal such as wanting to grow the business and needing to improve leadership skills to do so. The same principles apply. You want them coming out of the back end being very positive.

This is where your expertise and your experience really count because sometimes the client isn't able to fully articulate the scale of the problem because they don't have much experience with it. That's why it's a problem for them - because they've not been through it before.

On the other hand, you've been through it before with other clients. So, for example, if they see infighting and lack of teamwork among their top team, they may be focused on all of the unpleasant and wasteful aspects of that reality. But what you've also seen from your experience is how when you do get a team working effectively together you get much faster implementation of projects and strategies are much easier to implement. You get new ideas coming out. Usually there's a whole extra set of things, either problems or good things, that come from solving that problem; because you have experience, you know that. Your experience and expertise definitely come to bear on all of your suggestions.

Of course, they may say "no." You might suggest, "One of the things I've seen with some of my other clients is when they finally managed to get their team working together, they also find x result. Do you think that would be the case with your team?" and they might tell you that no, that wouldn't be the case. Or they may realize that, yes, that would work for them as well.

You can't just assume that they will get the same benefits as your other clients. However, your expertise and experience are a way to help the client see the true reality of the situation rather than just the initial presenting problem. You can either help them to see that the situation is serious or your questioning may lead them to realize it's not such a big problem after all.

Suzi: That's equally as important because that's about getting to no, which will allow you to dig to the next level of whatever the next problem is.

Let's say for example you're talking to a CEO. He tells you that one manager in a department is having a lot of staff turnover. Then you might say, "Okay, great. Tell me about that department. What do they do? How many departments do they impact? What numbers are we talking about?" Let's say it's ten people in the department and over the last year, they had to hire eight new people because eight people have left for various reasons. Like a coaching conversation, you would just start to ask questions around the issue to take it apart. You would ask whether exit interviews were conducted and whether the previous manager experienced similar attrition. You would also address the financial issues, and try to get them to assign a number to attracting, hiring, and training new hires. You'd ask, "What does it cost you to replace one person in that department? Oh, it costs you $100,000 to attract and hire and train the people in the new position. Okay great, so that's $100,000 dollars and you had eight new people come on board in the last six months. That's $800,000 you just invested and they're not even productive yet. So how much do you think it's costing you in lost productivity?" In this example, the CEO might say, "When that department is up and functioning, it produces $10 million. You would want to point that without digging deeper, the impact of this issue appears to be at least $10.8 million.

You could say, "Now we're looking at a $10.8 million impact so far. What other impacts have we not talked about?" You keep going and you keep asking for dollar values. You want to get the CEO squirming in their seat a little bit. You want to keep going until you get to the point where they really get it (maybe for the first time), that they've really thought about it (because they likely haven't really delved into it the way you're helping them think about it) and see that there's a real impact to not solving this. Once it is clear that it's a $10.8 million problem, it becomes super important to them that it get solved because every month that goes by that $10.8 million problem is having an exponential impact to the bottom line, which directly impacts the stakeholder and the shareholders' view of the CEO themselves or the board's view of the CEO, not to mention any external exposure. With this clarity, the issue becomes important to their specific career, personally. That's the next place you go. You want to help them wallow in the pain of cost to the organization and then you want to start asking them questions like: "What does that mean for you? If we don't get this solved, what does that mean for you? What will the rest of the organization think of you? What would the board think of you? What would the media and the public think of you and the company? What is this doing to you, to your career? And what would it mean for your career if you solved it? How would you quantify that?"

Ian: I think that's where executive coaching is sometimes a little bit different and it's an important place to go. If you were selling a computer system, for example, you might just focus on the rational side. But as an executive coach, those issues are exactly what you will be talking about as a coach too.

A lot of the reasons the executive is making the decision is based on those more emotional factors and the personal factors to them. You've got to talk about those as well – a lot of what weighs in their decision and a lot of what's important to them. It makes sense to start with the rational factors and to make sure you really understand the size and the scale of the problem from a business and economic perspective, but you also have to understand the emotional side because that's why they really make decisions and that's what they're thinking about as they go through this. It's important to be open with your client and start that openness in the sales process itself.

Suzi: Delving into what the issue means to them personally as well as their credibility and their leadership role, on top of what it means to the organization is critical in getting them to yes - or no.

Ian: In this process you are also role modeling what it would be like to work with you. As we said, this isn't a free coaching session, but this particular aspect of it is a bit like coaching because you're having a discussion with an executive where you're going beyond the surface issues and you're helping them to make a decision or make progress through the way you coach. Your ability to address both the rational and the emotional and the political factors will mark you as someone who's insightful and someone they would like to work with. This is an elegant process because you're helping them to flesh out the problems, but you're doing it with understanding and empathy. You're not hammering them.

Suzi: If you're doing it right, you're elegantly leveraging your artful coaching conversation skills, so you're building the relationship throughout the sales process. You're not doing it from the perspective of manipulating or driving your agenda to get them to say yes to working with you on a big deal. You're doing it from a coach approach of being fully in service, genuinely and authentically in service to your client's clarity. It's really about helping them make the decision and you have no attachment whatsoever to whether their decision is a "yes" or a "no" in that moment in the sales process. Even though you're still managing and leading the macro level sales process, you're still, in that moment, committed to their clarity. You're completely okay with helping them get clear on a no as much as you're completely okay with helping them get clear on a "yes but not with you" and a "yes and, yes, you." All of those outcomes need to be okay with you as the coach, otherwise you can't drive this process authentically. You'll be driving it with manipulation, which is not effective.

The Benefit of Being Conservative

Ian: One of the words I like to hear myself say when I'm in this conversation is the word *conservative*, particularly when it comes to the economic side of it. When you're talking to a potential client and exploring how much it's costing them or how much they would get in increased revenue if they did something differently, I like to keep reflecting back the discussion to them. So I might say, "So, roughly you've got seventy-four people there and it's costing $8,000. But let's just be conservative for a second. Conservatively speaking, about how much do you think that would impact your bottom line?" Whenever you're quantifying things, it's best to be conservative because it sends a signal to your potential client that you're not trying to exaggerate things. You're not looking to make the numbers bigger just so you'll get the sale. You're looking to make a sensible business decision. So if you go for conservative numbers and the conservative numbers look as if it's worth doing, then your executive client will be confident to go ahead. If instead you said let's take an estimate on the high side, then they wouldn't have as much confidence in the numbers and they might begin to believe that you were just pushing the numbers to get them to buy.

If you're always very conservative then in fact you may find your potential client pushing the numbers up. You might say, "What if we could just get a conservative 5 percent improvement in that?" then they might say, "No, actually I think we can get 10 percent." If you try to push the edges on the upper limits, the client will be pulling you down and they'll get the impression you're trying to sell them. In short, be conservative and they'll trust you more.

Suzi: What's really important in this process is that you're proving your credibility as a peer of theirs while you're asking the questions. You're not asking soft, loose, heart-based, open-ended coaching questions. You're asking savvy business questions as if you are the CEO of a mega corporation as well, demonstrating organizational awareness, systems thinking, your acumen, and your knowledge and capacity as a leader. In that way the process of asking insightful questions they may not have asked themselves yet and helping them get decision-making clarity establish you as a peer and proves your credibility while building the relationship.

Ian: It's a subtle and valuable way of building credibility. The more overt you are to try and prove your credibility - "Look, I've done this, I've got these clients," - the more your client will feel they're being sold to. Smart questions are a better credibility builder. Sharing stories and examples from other clients you've served and asking if those situations apply for this client is better than listing all the clients you've served and all the great results you got with them. It allows the client to mentally apply your other successes to his or her own situation.

Illuminating Impact

Ian: This is one of the areas where preparation is really valuable for you. Some people are really good off the cuff and they can be sitting in a meeting and the minute a client talks about a specific area, they'll come up with a whole series of great questions to ask to explore the impact. For most of us though, a little preparation goes a long way. It's worth thinking through areas you typically work on with clients and the problems you help them with. What usually are the root causes of those problems that you've seen and experienced and what usually are the impacts and the contingent impacts for different problems?

Make sure you mind map that out or write it all out in a table where you lay out the problems you work on, the typical root causes and the typical impacts. If that's fresh in your mind when you go into the meeting, that means you're going to be much quicker in asking those follow up questions and in finding the real impact of the problem or finding the real issue, rather than trying to make it up as you go along in every conversation.

Being well prepared is something that can differentiate an experienced expert coach from a brand new coach. A brand new coach can ask simple questions. "What keeps you up at night?" and repeatedly ask the question, "What's the impact of that?" but it's an experienced coach that knows what some of the impacts as a result of previous experience and can therefore ask the client about that specific detail that will help the client say, "Oh yes, I haven't thought of that, but actually you're right, it does impact there."

Suzi: There are two layers in this value proposition. One is helping them really get a sense of what it's costing them and their organization dollar-wise. The other layer is that it helps you understand the impact or the potential impact of your work with them.

For example, if you, in this decision-making conversation, in this little, mini coaching conversation within the bigger sales conversation, if your client determines through your line of questioning that the problem that they're talking to you about is a $500,000 problem, then the next line of questioning is, "What would it be worth to them to solve the problem?" So if it's a $500,000 problem it might not be worth $100,000 for them to spend to solve it. But if it's a $500,000 problem, for sure they'll be able to spend $5,000 to $50,000 to solve it. Likewise, if it's a $400 million problem, then this may be out of your league as a single coach, unless you have a team of experts to leverage. You may not have a coaching solution that's $2 million that they'd be willing to spend to solve it. Part of what the value proposition does is help you get a very clear sense of the scope of the problem and the impact of it to see whether or not you're a good match for the work. So this conversation helps you as well as them. It helps them determine if it's the right problem and it helps you determine if this is something you want to work on or refer to someone else who will serve them better.

Ian: You may get lucky and be able to make $500 million worth of improvements on your own. But usually the scale of the problem indicates the scale of the solution needed. If it's a really, really big scale problem, it may need a big network of coaches to come in, or it may not be a coaching solution that's needed.

Suzi: Think about this: If you have a CEO, or any senior level executive, and they're staring down the barrel of a gun at a $30 million problem that they have to get solved, and they have only spent $10,000 and it is not solved, They'll have to face the music. They'll have to go up against the senior leadership as well as maybe the board or other stakeholders and explain why they have only spent $10,000 to solve a $30 million problem. It's going to be a black mark against them in their career if they don't spend enough to solve a big enough problem. This is important to understand because a lot of times as coaches we get caught up in our own scarcity conversation about money and think, "Oh, if I would regularly charge $10,000 or $25,000 for a coaching engagement, I couldn't possibly ask for more." This is where the value proposition conversation is helpful to you. Once you have an understanding of the scale and scope of the problem that the organization is facing and the impact to the executive's career, then there's an opportunity for you to see what kind of solution at what price point is really going to make a difference to this problem.

Ian: The other side to that is if the amount is too low, it may be a warning sign that you're not the right choice. I always have a 10 to 1 ratio in mind that I've used for nearly twenty years. So if a client is not going to get ten times the value over the cost of my coaching within one year, then I don't feel comfortable about taking on that assignment. I'm better off trying to find someone else who will get that high return on investment. Coaching is very dependent on them making changes and improvements, and it can often feel uncertain to them. They always discount the ROI made through coaching much more than they would with a more traditional investment. So if it's only a 2 to 1 return on investment, the client is going to be looking at that cost all the time when really they should be focusing on making the improvements and getting the results in their business. It's better if there's a really big ROI in there for the client. It just takes that side out of the equation and you can concentrate on working with them and getting great results rather than constantly worrying about are they getting value for money.

"Magical Phrases"

Suzi: Let me just give you a couple of magical phrases that you can use in these conversations. They are going to be similar to the ones you use in the coaching conversation. One of the magic phrases is "I wonder if" - "I wonder if it would make sense to work on this together" or "I wonder if solving this problem would really have the impact that you're thinking." Another magic phrase is "would it make sense?" - "Would it make sense to have this kind of a solution for this problem?" or "Would it make sense for coaching to be the solution. These magic phrases can really help you explore whether or not it makes sense to work together and will help you lead the conversation where you help them decide.

Let's review what you're addressing and how you're doing it: lead them to wallow in the problem; clarify the value, impact, urgency, and importance; assign a dollar amount to it; and clarify what it means to the organization and to their career. After all of that you're going to move them through the other side of the tunnel and help them get a sense of what's possible. This is where you do your magic as a coach and help them see the possibility of what *can* be done and the impact and scope of that - the value, the benefits, the gains, and the cost savings. And then the question is simply whether *you* are the right solution in helping them think it through: "Would it make sense for us to do this together? Would it make sense for this to be the approach? I wonder if this approach would work." You do that in collaboration with them in that conversation. That's what helps them mentally get to the second yes of working with you.

Of course you're not saying that you're going to come in and do this and that and solve the problem. That's what a consultant would do. In coaching, it's collaborative. "I wonder if we did this, if this would solve the problem?" or "I wonder if working this way would work for you?" or "Would it make sense for us to try this approach?" That's a collaborative yes as opposed to a forced yes.

Ian: It's not a transaction, it's a partnership you're entering into. Although we've talked about ROI, it's not an arm's length ROI where they're thinking, "I buy this from you and wash my hands of it and you'll do everything and I'll get the results." It's more along the lines of them getting the returns by taking the actions themselves, as in: "Okay we're going to enter into this together and I'm going to be the one responsible for getting the results." You'll get the sense for when that's the right time to enter into that conversation. It's basically when the case is proven for this being the right thing to do going ahead, then the time is right to ask your "I wonder if" or "would it make sense" question about working together. When the case is proven that action is required, it is the time to start using the magic phrases - *I wonder if* and *would it make sense*.

Suzi: When the case is proven it's in the "eye of the beholder." It's when your client determines it's proven, and you'll see it in their body language as well as in their eyes, and you'll also hear it in the things they say. They'll be ready to talk about actions and forward movement.

Ian: You see it with some people, but with others you may need to check in. It may feel to you as if there's an overwhelming case for going ahead, but you should check with them. You should just ask them the blunt question: "Okay, so to summarize, does it feel as if progressing with this and making those changes is the right thing to do?" Get confirmation and then you can move on and start talking about whether it's the right thing to do with you.

Suzi: Next we're going to look at knowing how to recognize the yes so you know when to move on.

Toolbox

Coach Approach to Clarify Client Issues and Shape Coaching Offer

In a sales conversation, if you use the coach approach to helping your client decide whether to work with you, use question strategies to figure out the real issue and to explore the impact of the issue and motivation to change. Help them clarify their decision process to get to the root of the issue and shape the coaching solution.

You'll be seeking two distinct yes responses throughout the conversation:

1. Is this the right problem or area to work on and is it important enough to them to solve it?
2. Is coaching the right solution and are you the right person for them to work with?

The Value Proposition Coaching Conversation

Questions to **Clarify the Issue**:

1. What is the greatest challenge you face right now?
2. What is the biggest challenge coming down the pike?
3. What are you hoping coaching can solve?
4. What did you think it would make sense for us to talk about?

Explore the Scale, Importance, and Impact of the Problem or issue to determine if it is a priority that should be addressed:

1. How deep, broad, big is this problem?
2. Where does it show up most?
3. What does it mean for you in your role?
4. What does it mean for the organization and its stakeholders?
5. Who else does this touch?
6. What is the impact to them?
7. How many people are involved? What's the impact of this problem?

8. What is this costing your organization?
9. What would it be worth to solve this?
10. What would it mean for you in your role, or for the organization if we solved it?
11. What are the most meaningful metrics around this?
12. If we don't get this solved, what will that mean for you?

Client Meeting Checklist

- ☐ Framing your intention for yourself and the client
- ☐ Set the context
- ☐ Establish peer status to create trust and rapport
- ☐ State the intended outcome of the meeting
- ☐ Listen for what they're dealing with
- ☐ Listen for and handle their objections
- ☐ Align for value
- ☐ Clarify value proposition
- ☐ Listen for when the sale has been made
- ☐ Ask for the business

Elements of Successful Client Meetings

Rapport Building

- Opening the dialog
- Establishing peerage
- Finding connections
- Getting the client talking about themselves

Building Trust

- Confirm your credibility
- Demonstrate your competence
- Model your integrity
- Essential mindsets

Questioning

- Finding out as much as you can about what they do and how they do it
- Past, present, and future based questions
- Seeking how you can be helpful to this person
- Exploring what's possible

Listening

- Obstacles to listening
- Your actions: Confirm, clarify, take notes
- What to listen for

Story Telling

- The purpose of stories
- What kinds of stories to tell
- When to use stories to escalate the sale
- How to develop powerful, relevant stories

Getting to the Second Meeting

- Reasons to come back
- Requesting the meeting and scheduling the meeting
- Escalating the sale
- Presentation and proposal design

CHAPTER 12

Stop Selling: Helping Your Client to Start Working with You

Suzi: In the coach approach, knowing where to stop in the sales conversation is an important concept because we are often so busy thinking about the next question that we want to ask or the next idea we want to share that we don't recognize they've already said yes, or even if they haven't said it, we need to be able to recognize when they're thinking yes. Part of what has to happen at the point in the conversation where you ask for the business (or even before you've asked for the business) is to slow down and start listening because if the sale has been made, you've got to stop working at it. It is possible that you could overdo it and end up talking yourself out of the sale by overselling. Overselling is what we call it when you don't recognize that the potential client is already in and you continue exploring whether it would make sense to work together. It's important to recognize when you already have the business and need to move toward setting up the contract and getting the procurement lined up.

Ian: Buying coaching services is not the same as buying a new smartphone where the more features it has, the better. Their willingness to hire you is based on their confidence that by working with you they'll achieve the intended results and outcomes they want, not based on individual features and benefits of the coaching or of you. Once that confidence is established, there's no need to keep adding to the conversation. If you keep adding to the reasons, it's going to start to sound like overhead. It's going to sound like more work and more money for things they don't necessarily want.

Furthermore, if you keep adding more reasons and benefits to working with you, then they may begin to wonder why you're trying so hard to try to sell them.

Adding all these reasons also adds mental complexity, and you want the matter to feel simple and clear to them. You want them to have a simple mental picture of the idea that "by working with this person I'm going to be able to achieve my goals". You need to listen and be quiet when you ask whether they are ready to proceed. If they don't say anything immediately, it could be because they're thinking about it. Don't immediately jump to fill the void with more reasons why they should be working with you. Pause.

Suzi: It's important to remind yourself during the pause to slow down and make sure you've actually asked for their business. Sometimes, they'll close themselves. They've reached the yes before you've even asked and might be eagerly saying something like, "When we start, we'll do this" or "I can start next week" or "Let me just clear it with my boss and we're good to go." You may not recognize those statements as yes, and that's why it's important to know when to stop.

Remember we talked about a no and two yeses. So you've gotten past the no, and you helped them clarify the yes that their specific problem will get solved, that you know what you are talking about, that the relationship will work, and that your collaboration will achieve results. Now it's the point in the conversation when you need to stop and check in with yourself about whether you need to ask a question to ensure they are on board or whether it is obvious from what they are saying that they are already on board.

Check with yourself. If you're not sure if they are on board, stop and ask the question as opposed to piling more dialogue on top of what could already be a decision. Listen for whether or not the decision has been made. It's an important part of helping them make a decision either way. Listen for whether the decision has been made or whether the value has not yet been made clear yet and there's more dialogue to be had.

Ian: It's okay to ask. It's okay to say, "It sounds like you're ready to move ahead with this. Is that right? If so, we should start talking about x, y, and z" where x, y, and z are the mechanics of going forward. (We cover a lot of the final elements of sealing the deal in the next chapter.)

Establishing Expectations

Ian: Potential clients take that initial meeting as an example of what it would be like to work with you as a coach. When coaches are a bit lacking in self-confidence or new to winning business, sometimes they get a little too subservient in those initial meetings. They may even think that being really nice and likable will get them hired.

Of course, that's not the case. The client is looking for someone to have peer-level discussions with them. One of the key things you need to do throughout the meeting is to challenge appropriately and collaborate with your client. Be sure to include direct, useful, and valuable insights where you can during the meeting.

Suzi: Part of what you're doing in the coach approach is helping them reach clarity about things, and to see through new eyes, so be direct and tell the truth. Be yourself, because the way you interact with a potential client in this initial meeting or the way you interact during the sales process should be an authentic and genuine reflection of how you're going to be with them in the coaching process. For instance, if you hear during the sales conversation something you would address in a coaching conversation (insight, observation, nugget of truth), don't hold back. Be yourself, don't try to be on your best behavior to get the sale. Don't try to be Super Salesperson to get the sale and then turn into Super Coach once you've gotten the sale. That's not going to be authentic. That dis-ingenuity, that disconnect is going to come through loud and clear, which will do more to compromise your capacity to get the sale than anything you could say in particular. It's not about the words it's who you're being in the matter and your mindset of being in service to your potential client. Bringing the coach approach into the business development process is about acting in a similar way as you would as a coach but recognizing that you're not there to coach to them, you're there to help them decide what's the best way for them to move forward in whatever their commitment is.

Ian: I think there's increasing evidence from the world of sales generally that a more collaborative coaching-based approach to sales meetings is effective. We're in a world today where clients have access to a more information than ever before, and people don't like to be sold. When you first meet a client, the chances are they'll have looked you over, they'll have already thought about what they may want to get out of things. They may have gotten the answer wrong of course, but they have already thought about it. They have already have looked up what coaching is, who you are, and so forth. When you have the first meeting, if you act subservient and say yes to whatever it is they ask for, you're not differentiating yourself or adding value to the discussion.

Some of the most recent research published on business-to-business sales, for example has highlighted exactly this finding. Raintoday.com did interviews of 700 buyers of business-to-business services, I believe worth over $3 billion. And they asked them to classify the differences between the people who were successful at selling to them and the people who weren't.

It turns out that the two big factors that differentiate between the winners and those who didn't are firstly that the winners brought into play new ideas and a new perspective. Secondly, the winners took a collaborative approach.

If you think about someone who brings new ideas and perspectives and collaborates with you, that sounds a lot like a good coach. The traditional salesperson routine of coming in and talking about features and benefits and being really nice is less effective these days. What's working instead is a collaborative approach to sales, which is a much closer fit to how coaches naturally operate, so we have an advantage.

A Coach's Strongest Skill

Suzi: The strongest skill that we have as coaches is our ability and sophistication with our listening skills. What's brilliant in the business development process and what's brilliant in this mutual collaborative exploration with your potential client is bringing those listening skills to bear. Most of your traditional sales people in sales jobs are not trained to listen at the same depth and robust richness as coaches. This is an advantage that we have in the sales process that we may have undervalued. If we look at how to leverage our strength as listeners, to be in a mutual exploration with our potential clients, we can use our coaching powers to help them figure out if it makes sense to work together. We often can go into a sales conversation thinking the point is to get the sale. That's not the point. The point is to be of service and to collaborate with your prospect.

Refer back to the Client Meeting Checklist in the toolbox at the end of Chapter 10. It walks you through an outline of things to include in this conversation. It's there to provide a road map or to highlight the conversational markers. The first thing you want to do is make sure that you are framing your intention, both for yourself and for your client. Remember, the intention is not to get the sale. The intention is to be of service to help them figure out if it makes sense for them to move forward working with you as their coach.

Then you must set the context, explain the point of the conversation and what we're here to talk about and that we're here to work together. You want to make sure throughout the whole thing that you are establishing peer status because that's what creates trust and rapport. If you're being subservient, as in "I'm just being nice to you so you'll hire me," that's not going to go over well. Particularly with the senior level executive, you've got to establish that you are their equal and that you have just as much leadership capacity and knowledge as they do - perhaps not in their industry or in their business, but that in your own realm, you are their peer. It's always useful to state the intended outcome of the meeting and listen for what they're dealing with and what might be in their way.

Suzi: Let's dive deeper into asking for the business. We call that the coach approach to sealing the deal, and it's the last stage to getting new clients.

You Have to Ask

Ian: Most coaches don't like to feel as if they're being salesy, and I think many hope that clients will say, "Yes, let's start working right now. Let's sign the contract." But of course, that rarely happens. You do have to ask for the business. I prefer to be straightforward and simple when it comes to popping the question. Rather than using any clever closing techniques or anything like that, which I think can come across as manipulative and feel uncomfortable. I usually ask a basic question about whether they're ready to start working together. I may say, "It feels like you're ready to get going with this, would you like to talk about how we can actually work together?" And, usually, they'll say yes.

Suzi: Sometimes it's not as formal as popping the question. You don't need to phrase it in a certain way. I think just casually figuring out how you would normally say it in normal conversation is the way to do it. I might even ask, "So when would you like to get started?" or "When does it make sense for us to begin?" Then we're into a scheduling conversation. Or sometimes I might simply ask, "What's our next step? Are we ready for a contract?"

Sometimes if it's super clear that they're ready, they reassert that they've chosen you and yes, this is the right thing, and then you can say, "Great, I see the next steps as..." You step into leadership mode and say, "I will send you a contract, here's what you can expect to see. Is there anything else that you would need to see or anyone else inside your organization who might need to be involved at this point?" There might be some other approvals that they need to get. This is where we would want to make sure that we've asked the question but also look at what else they need from their side or inside their organization. Do they need approval from a boss or a board? Is there something that they need to sort through on the financial side with the CFO of their organization or do they have to get alignment with human resources in some way? Is there a regulated procurement process that will require compliance measures?

Ian: You ask the questions that are appropriate to their organization as well. If you're talking to the chief executive of a medium-sized company, you probably don't need to talk to them about all these hoops whereas if it's a more junior executive in a larger corporate, they'd probably need to check with HR, finance, and so forth.

Suzi: At this point the mindset should be shifting from sales person to coach. From that viewpoint you are looking at collaborating on the nuts and bolts of moving forward.

Take the Leadership Role

Ian: You take the leadership role now to set expectations: "Here's what normally happens. These are the issues we have to sort out." You're sitting on the same side of the table really and planning how you're going to start working together.

Suzi: Once you've asked the question and gotten the yes, then you want to have the commercial discussion to work out the specifics of the paperwork involved. We'll turn our attention to paperwork and contracts next.

Toolbox

Knowing When to Stop Selling:

- You must know when to stop the coach approach conversation and move to the next phase of contracting and procurement.
- They've already said yes, made the decision, mentally committed to move forward.
- Slow down and listen to see if the sale has been made so you don't oversell.
- Ask if they are ready to proceed...then pause long enough to let them think about their answer.
- Listen for things they may say that indicate you've made the sale.
- Listen for whether they've already made a decision.
- If you're not sure, stop and ask them.
- If the value is not yet clear, continue to dialogue.
- It sounds like you're ready to move ahead, should we now talk about the next steps?

Not Saying Yes To Everything:

- Don't fawn over your client and acquiesce to everything in order to get hired.
- Prove your willingness to challenge your client as a peer.
- Challenge appropriately, and input useful and valuable insights in the conversation.
- Tell the truth. Share observations.
- Bring in your own experience.
- Share a directive or a challenge as you would in a coaching conversation. It will demonstrate how you'll be with them as their coach.
- Be yourself in the sales process, authentic and consistent with how you'll be as a coach.

Collaborative, Coach Approach Wins:

- The most effective way of selling across all sectors is a collaborative, coaching style approach.
- Collaborate through the entire sales process.

- Bring new ideas and new perspectives to your potential client.
- Listening is key skill of both coaching and business development.
- Be in a mutual exploration with your client.
- Be of service and collaborate with them to gain clarity about whether it makes sense to move forward together.

Using Magic Phrases to Help Move Things Forward

"I wonder if..."

Examples:
I wonder if solving this problem would really have the impact you're thinking?
I wonder if this approach would work?
I wonder if we did this if it would solve the problem? I wonder if working this way would work for you?

"Would it make sense..."

Examples:
Would it make sense for us to work together?
Would it make sense for coaching to be the solution?
Would it make sense to have this kind of a solution to this problem?
Would it make sense to have a combination of coaching and training?
Would it make sense to use this approach?

Or use them both at the same time:

I wonder if it would make sense for us to work on this together?

Brainstorm some of your own magical phrases based on what has worked for you before.

Worksheet for Sales Conversation Preparation

It's often helpful in a sales conversation to be able to share similar situations that others have faced. However, recall can be challenging in the midst of a sales conversation, so it's useful to prepare in advance.

Use the following chart to prepare for a sales conversation. In the first column list the typical client issues or goals you work on. Work your way across the chart, listing causes, impacts, and metrics for each issue. Use the chart here for reference. You can access the worksheets online at http://libraryofprofessionalcoaching.com/marketing/executive-coach-marketing-resource-centre/

Sales Conversation Preparation Grid

Issues I've Worked on Successfully With Clients in the Past	Typical Root Causes or Potential Causes of Each Issue	First Level Impact of the Issue	Contingent Impacts of the Issue	How to Measure or Quantify each Issue and Impact to Bottom Line

Preparing Your Questions in Advance of the Sales Conversation

Using the completed grid, think through the following:

1. Choose the top issues most relevant to this client. For each area, write down one or two questions you can ask to identify whether this is an issue for the client you'll be speaking to.

Issue	Question 1	Question 2

2. List questions you can ask to identify the potential causes of the problem.
3. List questions you can ask to identify any related issues.
4. List questions you can ask to identify the various impacts of the issue and how they measure that impact.

CHAPTER 13
Contracts and Agreements

Ian: In this section we're going to look at a key component of sealing the deal: contracts and agreements. You and your client have agreed in principle that you'll be working together, and now you need some sort of paperwork.

Suzi: Whether you use a letter of engagement or a more formal agreement or a contract, depends in part on how you have chosen to do business and in part on what your client organization requires.

Ian: Typically, large organizations have more formal processes that they may require you to follow. You may need to use their forms and invoicing, and you will need to ask your client to tell you both what those requirements are as well as to connect you to the right people in finance or procurement to move forward.

The Benefit of a Contract

Suzi: If you're just starting out as a coach and you don't already have a standard contract in place, of course, we recommend hiring an attorney to help you sort out your contract to make sure it works with the legalities in your particular location. But if you really just need somewhere to begin, the International Coach Federation has a model contract or template agreement that you can use as a starting point, but be sure to check in with an attorney in your locale as well.

Ian: Laws are different of course in different countries and different states, and you want to make sure yours works for you. The contract is like a backstop, and ninety-nine times out of a hundred, you won't need to rely on it. Nevertheless you want to make sure you're covered and it's also more professional to make sure you have that in place.

Suzi: It also can help you keep track of what was promised. Sometimes after you've worked with clients for nine months or a year and they're on to their second agreement with you, it's hard to distinguish what you're billing them for when you go and do the billing each month. Sometimes I'll go back to the original agreement and contract to remember what we said we were going to work on, and how we were going to do it. It can be a tool for navigating the engagement. Sometimes a client will come back after years and then you'll have a reference point to refresh your memory of the previous engagement.

Ian: Coaching is a flexible approach and you tend to be client-centric and focused on what you do. It's very easy in some ways to become distracted, sometimes in a good sense if it turns out that doing things somewhat differently from what was proposed works better and gets your client to where you need to get them. But it's wise to check back to your contract to make sure you're still within the boundaries of what you agreed to. If not, you need to go back and refine the agreement detailing how you will work together.

Suzi: Watch carefully if the scope expands in a way that ends up not being favorable to you. If you're doing much more than what was agreed upon and not being compensated for it, that could have a detrimental impact on the relationship if you don't have a conversation about that. You don't want to find yourself resentful in a coaching relationship.

Ian: Absolutely. It's great to be nice to your clients, but you have to make sure that the requests for a bit of extra time here and there don't become a regular habit and suddenly your ninety-minute sessions become two-hour sessions and then two-and-a-half-hour sessions and then all of a sudden they're getting you for half the price that you agreed upfront.

Confirming the Scope and Duration

Suzi: As you finalize the contract and agreement in conversation with you client, you want to specifically spell out the scope and duration of the coaching, asking questions to determine what's going to work best for them and what you're willing to do. You want to determine the location and frequency and format of the coaching and you want to finalize, the goals of the coaching and the style of the coaching that would serve them best.

Essentially you're looking to create clarity and confirm the norms of how you will work together. You want to address questions like these:

- How long will your sessions be?
- How many sessions will there be, and what will the frequency be?
- What will you be discussing in those conversations?
- What administrative points need to be spelled out up front? - Will they be paying on retainer? Will you be billing them monthly? Will you be swiping their credit card as you go? Do you take credit cards? Will they be paying by PayPal? Will it be checks that need to be handled through their procurement system? Will payment be via electronic funds transfer?
- What's the starting and ending date?
- Are you providing the coaching or do you need to specify another coach from your team?

All the details must be thought through and clarified with your client's agreement.

Define What's Beyond Scope

Suzi: You also want to have a conversation with them to create clarity for you and them about what you won't do as well as what you will. Detail what's out of bounds. An example that comes to mind is from a very large corporation I was working with, coaching a senior-level vice president. This particular lesson happened early on in my coaching career. Somehow the coaching relationship with this person became a situation where he was delegating management tasks to me. It was uncomfortable, and it took me a while to figure what was happening, because in my commitment to be of service to this client, I didn't realize that what he was doing was having me do certain management conversations and tasks for him, including leading certain meetings.

I'll never forget one team meeting he was leading and I was there to support him (or so I thought). He had fifteen people in the room, including outside vendors and internal partners and collaborators, and at one point he just stood up in the middle of the dialogue and said that he was going to hand the reins of the meeting to me and then he left the room. I was his de facto deputy, which was frightening, not to mention inappropriate for me as his coach. These are the sorts of boundaries you want to spell out. You are not there to become someone that they can delegate management tasks to, which is more of a consulting role; if you are a consultant as well as a coach, you want to make sure that you're spelling that out and distinguishing that early on.

Ian: It's very easy for a client to fall into that because often senior executives don't have a lot of people they can trust that they know are incredibly competent as well. If your coaching is going well, you're establishing this position of trust with them and they'll come to really value what you do. In those situations there's a natural tendency for them to think, "Well, I need someone to work with this. Oh, Suzi will do it." And you'll do it.

Senior executives are accustomed to delegating, so even when you assign them some homework or research, they may ask you to do it! And there can be many, many things that aren't appropriate in the relationship. This is a good time to open up an inquiry and exploration around why they wish to hand it off to you as opposed to doing it themselves; what are they afraid of? What are they avoiding? That's the segue into the coaching conversation.

Finalize the Details of the Relationship

Suzi: It's helpful to have a discussion about the role of their executive assistant (EA); if they have one and how closely they work with that person. You want to know how much they trust their EA, and whether you will you be scheduling through their EA or scheduling directly with them. You want to find out how important that person is and how much that person does for them. In some cases, the EA can be your best friend in terms of getting information or helping you navigate the organization or navigate the executive's calendar. You want to explore that in your seal the deal conversation.

You also want to share with them whatever your policy is for how much they can contact you in between scheduled sessions, and how they should do so. Do you want to be accessible by cell phone for quick questions between sessions? Do you prefer they reach you by email or text? Also you have to explore how open they want to be with others in their organization about the fact that they are working with a coach; do they want to explain you to the rest of their organization or to their team in any way? How do they want you to explain yourself if you're asked in the hallways of the organization who you are and what you're doing there? Will they be announcing to the team that they're working with you or is it something that they want to keep private? Along the lines of when you're walking through the confidentiality agreement with them, you want to differentiate with them the concept of a public agenda versus a private agenda. So what is it that they are working with you on that's nobody else's business? That's the deep trusting meaningful work of the coach and client versus what is it that they want to be sharing with any of their key stakeholders. You can ask them to start thinking through and identifying who those key stakeholders are so that you can help them and so that you yourself can begin developing the strategic relationship and influence in their organization.

Ian: It can be quite embarrassing to be seen to have a coach in certain cultures. Some people might be worried that it's a sign of weakness that they need a coach. In other cultures where having a coach or someone to help them is much more common, it's not embarrassing. But for some it can feel as if they're maybe a little bit weak. But you will be surprised at how often when people share that they have a coach it's actually viewed as a positive thing. I started working with an executive about two years ago who was hesitant at first to tell his team that he was working with a coach. When he finally broke the news, he reported back to me that they all said they were very happy he was working with someone, because the team recognized the challenges he was dealing with and saw it as a positive step. In reality it is often less daunting than the executive imagines it will be to tell his or her people about working with a coach.

Suzi: This conversation in which you are hammering out the details of your agreement is actually a great time to glean anything you can about the culture of the organization. You're looking for anything that can help you navigate through supporting them in your coaching agreement.

Another issue to listen for during this conversation is future sales opportunities. You want to keep looking at who they work with and for, how they work in their organization, who they bump up against that's a challenge for them. You're looking and listening for information and touch points and puzzle pieces that will help you serve your client, but you're also *always* thinking about and *always* listening for opportunities for future sales conversations within the organization. The secret of sealing the deal is that once you're inside the organization, you cut the sales process in half. You build your business while you're billing time, but you can't take your eye off that business development ball! It's that much easier and faster to get a deal to close when you're expanding the sale from within an organization as opposed to starting from scratch trying to find a client. You want to be looking for and listing for opportunities where you can be of service and add value and contribute inside the organization once you've already landed a lead with one of the clients. This is an area coaches often overlook so pay attention to the opportunity to scope out future work rather than thinking your sole focus is now the current engagement. Always continue the sales conversations, even while you're serving the client.

Ian: And you're looking at this point as well to sow the seeds with the client that later on, when your work is going well together, when you're delivering great results for them and they're getting huge amounts of value from working with you, that you will be asking them for referrals. You will be asking them for introductions so that when you reach that point later on, it won't be a surprise. They know it's coming and their brain has a chance to, over time, think of the different people they can introduce you to. We mentioned this right back when we spoke about referrals. You're just sowing the seeds very early on, "By the way, as you know, I met you through a referral." assuming that was the case of course. "I do my business by referral. A bit later on, when we've been working together for a while and you're getting results from working with me, I'd just like to ask you to introduce me or give me the names of some people you think I'd also be able to do some great work with. You don't need to do it now but I just wanted to make you aware that's what I'll be asking in future."

Suzi: In our segment on referrals, we talked about how you can even put something in your contract about referrals - language that says that you will be asking the client at some point about referrals and that they always have the complete permission to accept or decline that request. It's just another way to plant seeds by using the contract itself.

Toolbox

Checklist of Topics for Sealing the Deal

Topics to cover when discussing the practical details of working together with regards to contracting and commercial protocols, paperwork, and administrative details:

Links* to two model contracts you can use as starting point (one from Certified Coach Federation and one for members of the International Coach Federation), but consult a lawyer in your location or industry that you coach in to make sure your contract is legal:

http://certifiedcoachesfederation.com/documents/Sample_2_Coaching_ Agreement.pdf (Or, use the shortcut to this link: http://bit.ly/ccfcontract)
ICF members can login to see this one: http://coachfederation.org/members/tools.cfm?ItemNumber=1776 (Or, use the shortcut to this link: http://bit.ly/icfagreement)
* Links accurate as of April 2016

1. What is their procurement process?
2. Who should you talk to in finance or procurement or HR to get set up in their system?
3. What will be the scope of the coaching?
4. What will be the duration of the coaching?
5. What will be the location, frequency, and format of the coaching?
6. What are the goals of the coaching?
7. What style of coaching will serve best?
8. What administrative matters need to be sorted out?
9. What are the payment methods - purchase orders, check payment, credit cards, PayPal, EFT?
10. What's out of scope that you won't be doing? Spell out boundaries.
11. Distinguish and clarify coaching versus consulting roles if you play both.
12. Who is their executive assistant, and how do they work with that person?
13. Who will you work with to schedule time?
14. Share policies and how to contact you.
15. How open they will be with their organization, team, and so forth about working with a coach?
16. Provide a confidentiality agreement.

17. Who are the key stakeholders?
18. What else do you need to know about their organization to navigate the engagement?
19. Plant seeds for referrals.
20. Communicate a termination strategy and exit plan for ending the engagement.
21. Set the stage for next steps to help them succeed on their own beyond coaching, including models and structures for support.

CHAPTER 14

Pricing

Suzi: The biggest piece that needs to get nailed down in this conversation with your client (and it might be several conversations) is the pricing. Let's take a look at some ways of approaching pricing.

Ian: I think a lot of coaches make a mistake with their pricing when they start out. They often price too low. They don't realize how much of their time they're going to spend coaching and billing versus how much of the time they're going to spend on marketing, on improving their own sales, on building the strategy, on other forms of promotion, on pro-bono work, and just the administrative side of the business or travel to the client. Setting your pricing isn't just a matter of taking your previous salary when you had a job and dividing it by the number of days in the week sort of thing. There are a couple of ways of thinking about it more strategically, which we'll explore now.

Target Revenue

Ian: When you are thinking of pricing, you need to know the minimum amount you are prepared to work for. That's based on your target revenue, which you need to figure out based on your target lifestyle and tax rates and business expenses. Then if you work on an assumption that even when you're an experienced coach and have a steady book of business with lots of referrals coming in, you're at most going to be working four days a week. More likely, when you're a start-up coach, you're going to working two or three days a week in terms of doing actual coaching. Let's say three days a week.

I'm talking about billable work, of course. Really early on, you're probably going to be working seven days a week to get things going, but in terms of billable work let's say at most three days a week early on. What you then do is you take that target revenue and divide it into the three days a week and you come up with a figure that could be a daily rate or an hourly rate. The thing to bear in mind is that's the minimum. We're not saying that's how you calculate your fees to clients, but you want to have that figure in your head as a minimum you need to earn.

Ideally of course you'd like to earn more than that. How much more than that you can earn is dependent on the value you're delivering to your clients as well as your competitors' rates. The more established you are, the stronger the reputation you have, the more you stand out in your field, the less you have to worry about the comparison to competitors' pricing. It's a matter of what value you are delivering to your clients and the minimum rate you're prepared to work for.

If there's a gap in between those two - if the rate you can charge to clients because of the value you're delivering and the market rate is significantly higher than the minimum you need, that's great. That means you've got a decent range to set your prices in. Now if your minimum rate is higher than the value you are delivering to your clients, then there's no return on investment for them so that won't work. But as long as your minimum rate is below the value you're delivering to your client, or to put it better, the value that you're delivering to your client is much higher than the rate you want to charge, then you can pick a rate somewhere in between there.

Pricing Structures

Ian: How that translates into pricing for the client then depends on how you want to bill. There are some people who will just quote an hourly rate or a rate per session. My own preference is to charge a fixed monthly fee for working with me, which usually includes two sessions a month. Now if we spend a little bit less or a little bit more time on the session or they only have one session, it's the same monthly rate every month. It's almost like a retainer, a monthly fee for working with me. It means they don't have to worry about me being "on the clock" all the time and I find it doesn't get abused because my clients are just as busy as me. They don't spend half their day on email asking me questions all the time.

In other cases, you could charge a project-based rate if that's the sort of coaching you do. If your work with clients is always done in three months, or if for a particular client you can see that in three months it could be done and dusted, then you can charge one fixed fee for that piece of coaching work. That could work well for them because especially when they go through finance to get approval, there will be a fixed budget rather than an open-ended number that could go on forever. Pricing on a fixed basis can work well for clients and their finance teams.

Suzi: I have a couple of ways of thinking about pricing. Sometimes I factor in value when I'm creating the price. Meaning you think through the value, basing the pricing on the value that the clients will get, or based on what the client has said the value would be during your value proposition conversation that we previously covered. Sometimes the pricing is based on the market norms, so I'm not going to go in charging $150 per hour if I'm working with a senior level executive who's accustomed to paying $795 per hour to their attorney. You want to base your price on market norms for your level or industry of client. Then there's another factor, which is pricing based on your unique expertise or knowledge or experience. After being in business for over twenty-two years, I have experience, expertise, and knowledge. I have degrees, and I've authored books. There's also a certain amount of demand on my time. All of these components factor into the pricing as well. There's also knowing your willingness to adjust price based on other considerations, such as how much work you're willing to do pro-bono, how much work you're going to do for discounted rates and for whom and why. That way, when discounts are requested, or when someone has sticker shock at your price, you can determine if this is a client or situation that fits for you to offer at a reduced rate or pro bono.

Going back to what you're saying, Ian, I liked your point about how you think about it from the target revenues that you want to create in a year then backing it up from there. Another way to think about it is the target number of clients that you can fully serve. The reality is that one-on-one coaching is not easily scalable. You're one coach and you have twenty-four hours in any given day and there's not much you can do to change that. You can scale the business in other ways through products or other services or other people working for you, but at the core, there are time constraints. There are limits to how many people you can coach and coach well, and how much time you want to spend with each of them. You also have to factor in travel time, if that's an issue, or if you coach by the phone and can stack clients up back to back by phone. All of that has to get factored in and you don't want to set yourself up for a loss. You want them to match. If you do your revenue target and it turns out that you have to coach forty-five people a week, that might not necessarily work and you might have to shift the number to get that minimum dollar amount because you know that you truly can only serve twenty clients a week.

Ian: It's an important sanity check to make sure the number of clients you're looking to get is a viable number, meaning realistically how many clients you could fit into your schedule. If the numbers don't come out right, you'll have to rethink the model. That's one of the reasons why it's worth going through the exercise of considering your target revenues. If you think it through and come up with a weekly number of clients that is just not doable, then you need to think through your pricing levels. They'll need to be higher in order for you to survive. Or you might have to rethink your revenue targets.

Suzi: You also have to consider how much you want to work. It's not just about survival. What's your ideal balance in life? How much do you want to be working and how much do you want to be earning? What are the different ways you can accomplish that? How many clients do I need to get at my fee rate to earn that amount, and do I really want to coach that many people in one week? The math might indicate, for example, that to earn what you want, you'd need to coach more clients than you could fully devote your energy and presence to in any given day. The joy of this business is that there is a lot of flexibility.

Just to share some different ways of thinking about the models; I've known people who charge an hourly rate, some people offer a daily rate, and Ian does a monthly rate. I do a six-month engagement rate and twelve-month engagement rate because I'm trying to incentivize the long-term relationship. We do some project-based fees or retainers but I also have an hourly pay-as-you-go rate for those people who have already been through a six-month or a twelve-month engagement with me and want more but they don't another long-term engagement. They want some monthly check-in calls or they want some ad hoc check-in calls so we have an hourly rate for that.

Ian: In that case, you can put a cap on it. It's either an hourly rate for one-off sessions or a monthly rate where they can take up to about this amount of time, but if it goes over two hours or four hours (or whatever amount you choose), then you need to renegotiate how much that's going to be.

Suzi: But it also depends on you and how accessible you want to be. I did hear of a story about a woman who charges an up-front fee, an annual fee of $180K, to allow clients to be in a VIP category where they have access to her anytime, meaning she will take their call anytime they call. They're paying this upfront fee just for the right to have that level of access. I thought that was interesting, but it would not work in my lifestyle because I do most of my coaching by phone so I stack the calls back-to-back and everybody is scheduled. I don't have time in between to just drop everything and handle emergencies that come up.

You've got to figure out what's going to work for your lifestyle, revenue needs, and work-life balance, and how much you can really do to serve your clients best. There are various things to juggle when you're creating your pricing. And of course all of this thinking on pricing happens before you're having seal-the-deal conversations.

Fee Increases

Ian: I have a mental rule that I use that has proven quite helpful: Whenever I get certain number of clients at my current fee level (for instance, if I get ten clients at one fee level), I automatically put up the fee level by 10 percent. It's a hard and fast rule. It's all mechanical and it stops me from worrying year after year about what my pricing should be. I know if I get ten clients at one level, I increase the pricing by 10 percent automatically. The logic is that if I'm getting ten clients then obviously people are willing to pay that price, so let's put it up by 10 percent and see if the next ten clients are willing to pay that price. Eventually, you're going to hit a ceiling, and that will be the pricing level that reflects the amount that people value you on average. As you become more experienced and better known in your field, more clients will come to you and you will be able to charge more.

Rather than trying to guess it every time, I like this mechanical rule which takes away all the pain and the mental anguish over pricing. The price goes up after every 10 clients by 10 percent. That's the rule. Eventually I may be at point at which no one is willing to pay the amount it's gone up to, so I'll have to ratchet it down again, but it hasn't happened yet and it makes things nice and simple.

Suzi: This raises an important point about not having different prices for every client, even if they ask for different pricing. There should be a general norm in your pricing otherwise it becomes an administrative hassle on your end to price everybody differently. I've heard of coaches who have one price for their executive clients at a certain level and a lower price for mid-level managers and a lower price for line staff, and then they even have a lower price for people who are paying out-of-pocket personally, when their organization is not paying for the coaching. These people also have a whole different set of pricing for nonprofit organizations or government. You can go crazy with a different price for every client. Even if you do end up making discounts for certain clients for reasons that make sense all around, you still want to have your base rate, which is your price that you know is your price that the market will bear and that serves you, serves the client, and generally works well for everybody. If there's the occasion where it makes sense for you and you're willing to discount it, great. But really for your own sake, you don't want to have different pricing for everybody.

Ian: I find if you give different pricing, then you will always run into the situation where someone says "not quite now" and then they come back in three months or six months and of course you forgot how much you quoted them at that time. It just gets into a nightmare. The administrative system to manage all the different pricing level is too complex.

There is a school of thought that says you should be pricing a bit like if you're pricing a consulting project or a construction project where the price of what you do is related to the value the client gets.

That's a nice model to use for big one-off projects like in consulting where you're doing something different every time. That pricing is more a reflection of the value you're delivering and it allows you to have a higher rate by delivering more value.

I found the best way to get to a similar point when it comes to coaching is just to price high anyway based on delivering a lot of value and then your market self selects. You end up only working with the people for which that high price is a good value and who can afford it.

One of the dangers of charging on a case-by-case basis - charging x for executives of large corporations and half of x for people in smaller corporations and two thirds of x for people in medium-sized organizations - is that you might end up working all the time with people in smaller corporations and you wouldn't be making the revenue that you wanted and you wouldn't be delivering the value to the world that you could. It is best to pick the price that you want, in my experience anyway, and then work for the organizations where that's a great price for them. This is more effective than going downmarket and having a cheaper version of yourself for smaller organizations.

Now by all means if you want to do some kind of lower price for nonprofits or people paying out of their own pockets then that's fine. Just try to keep the model as simple as possible.

Planning the End Game

Suzi: One of the last points to keep in mind during the conversation where you're actually sealing the deal with the client is to look at the end game. How do we end our work together? Is it a termination strategy or a more gradual exit strategy? You want to talk that through so that the expectations are clear and you perhaps may even have that in your letter of agreement. Something that I found really successful in setting the stage for how you're going to end your work together is reassuring them that you're not merely going to end with a proposal for more work or for add-on work, but that your commitment is to set them up to succeed on their own without you and that you'll help them create their plan for support for self-coaching going forward after they are done with you. You both want to know that you're not going to walk away and leave them high and dry but you're also not going to be stringing them along for years on end either. There's a completion plan that's discussed at the starting point just so that you know what matters to them and you can plan accordingly.

Ian: I think that's a nice way of doing things because it reminds you to do it because it's in the contract and it forces you in the last two or three sessions to work specifically on that plan for how they are going to become self-sufficient and build their support network, rather than just leaving them abruptly. This doesn't mean you won't check back in with them or won't coach them again if needed, but building that transition to self-sufficiency into your plan is valuable.

Suzi: Oftentimes, even in thinking through the coaching plan with them, they will realize they don't want to do it on their own, and that becomes your next engagement. It can work as a business development strategy as well but not if it's done as a gimmick or technique to get more business. It truly has to come from a commitment to helping them self-sustain beyond your work with them.

Ian: You'll get there and then it's their decision. It's not just reaching a hard stop and then the client panicking and thinking, "Oh, I need some more." It's that you work with them in becoming self-sufficient and they may decide for themselves, "Actually, this is not for me. I'm not ready yet. I need some more coaching" or "Yes, this is brilliant, I am now set up and I can continue on my own." It's a considered decision on their part, rather than a panicked reaction.

Suzi: And they still come back a few years later. That happens all the time.

Toolbox

Pricing Models and Factors

1. What is minimum amount you're prepared to work for?
2. What are my target revenues?
3. What is my target lifestyle?
4. What are typical expenses in my business and what are the taxes?
5. What kind of rate do I want to charge?
6. How many days per week do I want to be billable?
7. How many clients will I need to get at my preferred rate to get to my target revenues?
   - Example: Target revenue ($$) divided into three days per week, gets you a daily rate, you can divide by the number of hours you'd like to work per day to get hourly rate. That's your minimum.
   - Ideally, you'll want to earn more. How much more you earn depends on value you deliver to clients, rates of competitors, reputation strength, distinction you have in the field.
   - Ensure value you deliver to your client is much higher (10x) than your rate.
   - Figure out how you'd like to charge: hourly, by session, daily, monthly, three-months, six-months, annually, project-based fixed fee, retainer.
   - Your rates are also based on value, market norms, and your unique expertise/ knowledge/ experience.
8. How much pro-bono work do you want to do per year and for whom?
9. How many people can you work with and truly serve well at any given time (day or week)?
10. Is the number of clients you're trying to get a viable number?
11. What is ideal balance in life: how much do you want to work to earn how much revenue?
12. How accessible do you want to be?
13. How much total revenue do you want to come from coaching?
14. At what intervals will you increase your rates?
    - Example: If I get 10 clients at current rate, then I'll increase rate by 10%
15. Pricing should be consistent so you don't have different rates for every type of client.

16. Set your base rate and then you can offer discounts for various reasons.
17. During your business development process, track the rates you quoted each client, in case they don't close now, but come back later.
18. Err on the side of pricing high and delivering enormous value to the organizations where that value is great for them.

CHAPTER 15

Growing Your Business

Ian: This final section is focused on how to sustainably and systematically growing your business. So far we've looked at how to define who the right clients are for you, how to find those potential clients, how to initially connect with them, how to have that sales conversation with them, help them decide and finally seal the deal so you've brought on paying clients. In this section we're going to cover a couple of topics about how to grow from there in a sustainable and a systematic manner.

We're going to cover four main areas: what you can do *when* you're working with a client that helps to keep growing your business sustainably; what to do *after* you've worked with a client; building your market presence long-term so clients can find you; and getting support and help so you can focus on the important elements that are going to help your business. Those first two areas are going to sound a little bit like just good customer service. Of course, having great customer service, delivering great value to your clients, building relationships with them and others in the organization while you're there is the foundation to growing your business while you're billing time. It's not a separate activity.

Building Your Business as You're Working

Suzi: You can build your business when you're working with someone by working from a baseline of excellence - providing excellent service. That's the expected norm at this point. You cannot expect to grow your business sustainably or otherwise if you are not really hitting the mark and providing excellent service, excellent value, exceeding customer expectations. Consciously creating an exceptional customer experience is not just great for the client, it's good for you too because it's really helpful in growing your business.

To build your business as you're working with someone, you also want to let your client know at different points throughout the engagement that you will be looking for more work. That might look like asking them for referrals within their organization, or asking for introductions to other people in their organization. Perhaps it's being mindful while you're doing interviews on behalf of your executive within their organization that you're talking to people who could be potential clients. If they say something in the interview that leads you to believe there is an opportunity there, communicate that transparently back with your client as well. The goal is to constantly be planting seeds for expanding your business while you're working with the client. Seek referrals not only in their organization but external to the organization as well with people that they know in their network. You want to be in an ongoing networking relationship while you're work with the client.

Ian: Transparency is the key here. I know some coaches who struggle a little bit with extending current relationships. Often the root cause is that they haven't spoken transparently with their clients at the start. They haven't said that they're going to be looking to get referrals or extend their relationships with the client's organization. As a result, whenever they spot opportunities downstream and they're speaking to people and thinking, "This could be a great client for me," they feel guilty that they didn't communicate in advance that they might be requesting referrals. The issue then escalates in their mind to a point where they can't possibly talk to these people and build a relationship because they think it would be wrong since they are working with the existing client. Transparency circumvents all of those weird, guilty feelings. Of course if you inform your client at the start that you'd like to work with more people in their organization and the original client says they wouldn't feel comfortable with that, then you'll have to respect that and figure out what it means for you. But at least nine times out of ten they're not going to mind at all.

Suzi: Another opportunity for building business while you're working with someone is building into your process a "lessons learned" conversation at the mid-point and end point of the engagement. This conversation is an opportunity to reflect on the coaching engagement to see how far you've come or to see if you've gotten the results that you want, to see what's working well for the client or what we can improve upon in the future. What's really powerful in the coaching approach is that these conversations generally become a celebration of your client's success. Your client is so happy with what's been happening that they share their appreciation for you. That's the perfect and natural time to ask for a testimonial.

There's some artfulness to asking for a testimonial. In some relationships you can just say, "Great, would you put that in a testimonial that I can use?" In other contexts, you might be better served by taking notes of what they're saying they accomplished and about the value of the coaching in their own words and what specifically they appreciate about having worked with you. Then feed it back to them and ask if you can quote them. That way writing a testimonial doesn't seem like another item on their to-do list.

The "lessons learned" conversation is not only excellent customer service but it's a powerful vehicle for business development - creating a systematic and sustainable way of getting business by having that conversation. When you're having that conversation and you find out how great everything is, how much they love working with you, and how they're getting these great results, you can ask, "Is there anyone else that you think would benefit from the same sort of thing we've been doing? Is there anyone else in the organization that we should be talking to? Is there anyone on your team that you think could benefit from this?" These are natural questions to ask in that context, rather than feeling the need to set up a separate sales conversation.

Ian: One of the secrets to that is awareness - looking out for what's going on in the client's business generally, their organization, their wider industry, and sector. If you really pay attention and care about the client's organization and what's going on, you'll be more aware of the challenges that they're going to be facing. That allows you to ask valuable and intelligent questions as a lead into business-level conversations that introduce areas into the discussions that you can maybe help them with. These conversations position you as being knowledgeable and interested and helpful outside just the areas you've been coaching them on. This begins to position you as a business-level peer - the trusted advisor role that ideally you'd like to get with many clients. As you speak to people in their organization, become aware of who might have a real need for coaching so that when you have that "lessons learned" conversation, you can say, "While I was speaking to so and so, I noticed this." That way you're not putting all the responsibility on them to identify other potential clients in their organization.

Suzi: In addition to assisting your client in cultivating their own strategic relationships of influence, you want to be looking at who are the key stakeholders and who are the folks that are strategic for you in the organization to be building relationships with. Then asking your client for introductions to their peers or colleagues so that you can, perhaps, build it into the system in terms of 360-degrees feedback. There are times when not only are you gathering valuable data for your clients from their peers and colleagues, but you're also building those relationships or at least planting the seeds for those relationships for yourself. There's an opportunity inside that context when you're interviewing for 360-feedback. You can say, "I am coaching this executive for six months, and I'm on deck to help them create a new level of excellence in their leadership. One way we achieve that is by gathering feedback from people who are important to them and have insight to their growth opportunities and their strengths." This is a great way to start to build relationships. You gather the feedback but in the course of gathering the feedback, you can conversationally develop relationships with other strategic key influencers that could possibly turn into business development conversations later. The 360 interviews are an opportunity to demonstrate your own executive presence and gravitas and understanding of the corporate world.

Ian: It happens naturally anyway when you're interviewing these people and you're doing 360-degree feedback or any other meaningful or substantive interaction with them, because you're asking deep and powerful questions of them. Of course, this relationship building happens even faster and even better if you think about it and plan it beforehand. But it comes back to transparency from the start and making sure that you and your client have discussed that as a great by-product of the work that you're doing, you could build relationships with others as well. You primary focus is getting the 360-degree feedback for your client's benefit, but it has a positive side effect for you too.

Suzi: It's also about seeking different ways that you can add value beyond what's contracted. For example, I'm coaching with a senior executive and the HR person in the organization is very much an advocate for coaching. She wants to be supportive of the coaching and facilitate and help the coaching, yet there's no time built into the contract for me to be spending hours in conversation with this HR person. However, I'm doing it because it adds value beyond what was contracted for and it builds a relationship that could potentially be strategic. Also, the more trust you build with other folks, the more candid insights you get about the person you are coaching. They let down their guard and they don't try to be as politically correct anymore, and then you get the real down and dirty.

Ian: I think that's part of a more general principle. If we're looking at the sales cycle and how long it takes to bring in a new client, the fastest way to shorten a sales cycle is for it not to be a cycle. It's for you to be working on it all the time. So whenever you're in an organization, 10 percent of your brain all the time is looking for these opportunities, looking for people to talk to. Occasionally, you'll sit back and do a little analysis and think about who the strategically important people are to map out who you might want introductions to. If you do this on an ongoing basis, you may avoid the panic mode when the engagement ends and you're wondering where your next client is coming from. You'll have a backlog of relationships and opportunities in place that you can go to next.

Suzi: If you don't do this you'll end up with something like a six-month lag because it takes some time to build. If you're not working on business development all the time while you're billable, then you're going to create that up-and-down cycle - the peaks and troughs - that many coaches face. In the moment it may seem a surprise to you, but actually it's predictable. If you focus solely on delivering coaching services to your current clients, when those end, you will need to start the whole business development cycle from scratch if you're not doing it at the same time as serving your existing clients.

By employing the coach approach to being systematic and sustainable about building your business while billing time, you can generate a more predictable income and a steady stream of business all the time ready for when you're available. This also enables you to avoid that aura of desperation, or neediness, or attachment to getting a client, which is a turn-off for most clients and prevents them from buying your services. When you're very busy, your energy is that of service and success, which is very attractive to buyers. They want the social proof they imagine is there by virtue of your relative unavailability.

Ian: When you're desperate, you also try and push them faster than they want to go. But the reality is that things always take longer than expected. When you try and push people faster than their natural timeline, it pushes them away rather than bringing them toward you. But if you're busy and working, it is easier to go with the natural timeline toward engagement.

What to Do after You've Worked with a Client

Ian: After an engagement is finished, don't lose touch with that client. If you haven't already secured testimonials during the engagement, the end is a great time to capture the success in their words. Ideally you've already talked to them about transitioning to self-coaching or being able to do things themselves, but you'll schedule something to go and check back in and make sure they're doing okay. At that point they might request more support or they might be doing brilliantly. Regardless, these are opportunities to speak with them, continue to build the relationship, and continue to add value over and above what you are originally contracted for. And, of course, it may emerge that there are other ways you can help them, either a new challenge or revisiting the work previously completed. Or at that point you may get a referral or introduction to other people in their organization during that post-engagement period when you're not working with them fully anymore but you are still keeping a good relationship with them.

Suzi: It's really just letting them know that you're thinking about them even though they're not paying you at the moment. It's that human connection piece. Let's say you come across some article or a video that resonates with a conversation you had with them, even if it's years ago, they'll love to hear from you. If you set up Google Alerts to tell you about the companies that you coached in, sometimes you'll see news bits about them come around and you can comment on it. After you're done working with them, you can email them back saying, "Hey, I saw this bit about the CEO stepping down, what does that mean for you and your role? Does it make sense for us to have a conversation? I just want to make sure you're okay." These are things you would normally do to extend empathy and care for another human being. If you systematically create ways to follow up with past clients and find these opportunities to reach out and connect, you'll never know what will open up as a result. The bottom line is it is just nice to do to sustain the relationship, but a few years down the road, they could come back to you for more coaching or think of you when someone they're talking to needs coaching.

Ian: Some people object to that systematic relationship building, to using tools to help them; they think it's not "real." But the truth is that in setting up a system, you're just making sure that you're going to actually do the things that you wish you would do. You want to do these things anyway: following them, helping them out, keeping in touch, adding value, just having that personal element. You want to do it, but if you don't systematize it with things like Google Alerts or notes in your calendar or your CRM associated with this contact, you'll get so busy with other client work that you won't do it. Using a system makes it easier and ensures you do the kind of follow-up you want to do.

Suzi: This is also about tracking results. Over time as clients come back to you, you'll be able to see the results of your efforts. You'll see which clients are coming back and why and if they are clients that you're keeping in touch with, then you can begin to assess what is working for you in the customized business development system you're creating. You want to be able to tweak the experiment as you go to learn what leveraged activities yield the best results. How are you going to know what's working if you're not tracking it? You want to test the feedback too. Are you bothering people? Are you emailing them too often? This is not about a cookie-cutter system. It's really about honoring your personal way of staying connected with your clients and tracking the results of that. That's really all we mean when we say "system" - your own personal ways of keeping track of your activities that works best for you.

Building Your Market Presence Long Term

Suzi: Even when you are very busy with clients, you must keep marketing and actively looking for ways to nurture the relationships. If you think back to the first chapter where we talked about 100 to 1 ratio (your ratio may be different), it is clear that you constantly need to meet and connect with a lot of potential clients. You'll be kissing a lot of frogs if you want to turn some of them into princes or princesses downstream. You need to keep doing that on a consistent basis.

Make sure you're tracking the numbers. How many new people are you getting in contact with? How many of those are turning into meetings to talk about potentially working together? Tracking those numbers is going to help you make sure that you don't get complacent. It will help you avoid that awful moment when you complete an engagement and realize you haven't got any new clients lined up. It also means you won't get too drawn into the really exciting, interesting client work you're doing because you will reserve time to keep working on your marketing.

It's really discipline in the opposite direction. It's not the discipline of what to do when you don't have enough clients keeping you busy. There's a discipline the other way - not letting yourself get so fully booked that 100 percent of your time is billable and you don't have any time left for marketing. It should be built into your model, whatever you design that works for you. Maybe you have a dedicated day for marketing or maybe you have two mornings a week or maybe you figure out a way to put fifteen minutes in each day. You're looking for whatever works for you so that you have dedicated time. If you are too busy, then your marketing activities will fall by the wayside. But no one can afford that long term. That is why you always have to be building and sustaining your visibility in the marketplace; you can't only do it when you need new clients. This happens in a number of different ways - through branding, PR, writing books and articles, and creating products for your business or opportunities for visibility for yourself that will then create what we call "inbound marketing" (meaning the clients are now coming to you instead of you always having to hassle to find them).

Ian:As your business becomes more mature and you get busier and busier, you will likely shift to this creation of products and raising your visibility for inbound marketing. As you're starting up and growing your business, you're doing a lot of the marketing and business development face-to-face. That's always going to be the fastest, most secure method: to leverage personal relationships, get referrals, and use that personal touch and credibility. But as more and more of your time goes into actually doing the client work, you're going to have less time for marketing. You may be in a completely different location where you can't do face-to-face and you're going to need to rely more on other assets you've created that will raise your profile, raise your credibility and begin to bring people towards you without you having to take action to do so. Your website, articles, books, and video presentations allow you to demonstrate your credibility to a wider audience, and they all work day and night to bring people your way, which means you don't have to be physically present doing the marketing in real time. You are leveraging a portfolio or menu of approaches.

Suzi: It's about balancing the approaches that work for you. We're talking about a whole bunch of different things. We're not advocating that you make yourself crazy doing everything. Just think strategically about what works for you to systematically and sustainably grow your coaching business in a way that allows you to hit all of these points without making yourself. insane. If you're an extrovert, you probably are going to want more socializing and external time being with people. If you're an introvert, you probably are naturally going to want more writing time, social media time, or alone-in-your-room time on your computer. Be conscious of that. There's nothing wrong with honoring your natural frame of reference, but you also want to make sure that you have a balance. Over time you won't have to track it specifically. You'll start to have an intuitive sense of whether it's been too long since you met new prospective clients or were on social media or wrote a blog post. You'll start to just have a sense of where to put your energy next. Of course, if you're one who loves to schedule things and follow a predictable routine, then absolutely build a schedule for all the activities that generate real results for you so that you can confidently take consistent action.

Ian: In the early days I would recommend tracking how you are using your time. I found it very easy when I first started out to just get into the habit of going to networking events. I didn't even have to switch my brain on - Wednesday nights was one event, and Friday mornings, it was another. I put on my suit and went off to shake some hands talk to people. I also didn't really realize how much time it took. You should track your investment of time and money and whether you're getting results from that. In other words, is it working? Are you getting new clients? Can you track where those opportunities are coming from?

Be sure to track your time with social media. It's easy to think you'll spend ten minutes on a LinkedIn group sharing some ideas and then come up for air two hours later. It can actually feel more like leisure that it does work so you don't realize how much time you're putting into it. It's important to be aware of that time and measure what you're getting out of it. Measuring isn't easy, but when people contact you, it's worth asking them where they first heard of you. You want a sense of where people are finding you because it will help you get the best return on your investment of time. Sometimes it takes a while before you see that you're actually getting meetings from these actions. Give it time! On the other hand, if it's been many months with no results, it may be time to choose an alternative method.

Suzi: Over time there is a cumulative effect in terms of your market presence. All of these different little things reach a tipping point and people start to say, "I see you everywhere." That's when you know you're out there.

Ian: This is why it's important to maintain a balance early on. A lot of those activities - blogging, social media, writing articles, everything that will build your assets - won't necessarily pay off much early on. You might get lucky and someone might read the article, phone you up immediately and bang you've got a client. But often they take time to build, so that's why it's important to balance them with referrals and personal introductions and things like that which are going to pay off immediately. Over time you begin to get scale and people begin to see you in multiple places. What I found, for example, is that after I'd been writing online for a while and posting some things on other people's sites, people began to come to me to ask me to get involved in other things. Without me having to do a lot more work, suddenly I was being asked to take part in events and to write guest articles. That's what happens when you reach a certain level of visibility because of the time investment you've made. Then you get a snow-ball effect where you no longer have to push to get so many things out there. People are pulling for you to get hold of your material and things. Then you have different challenges.

Suzi: It's not about building fame. That's not the point here. It's really just about being visible and findable.

Ian: Fame is a tool for being found and to do the things that allow you to achieve your calling. There are some of us whose calling is to be famous. But for most of us it lies in other areas, and the fame side just helps people to find you so you get to do the things that you love doing and really help people.

Suzi: One of the metrics for how you'll know you're being successful at this (because people will not always answer your blog post or respond to your email so you don't always get immediate feedback that your efforts are working) is when you meet someone for the first time and they say, "Oh I've heard of you." That kind of thing is one metric that you're doing a good job of creating sufficient visibility. Now there is so much noise in the marketplace, both online and off, that it becomes more important to take actions that allow you to be found by your target market. Ian and I were talking about how you could, if you wanted to, literally spend twenty-four hours a day, every day, attending free webinars. People are putting so much valuable content out there for free and there is so much noise in the marketplace that it seems like it would be a Herculean effort to create visibility, but it really can be accomplished if it is done systematically and methodically over time. You don't have to worry about creating visibility overnight. It's baby steps consistently taken over time that will do the work for you.

Ian: I often compare it to someone who's trying to lose a little bit of weight this year. One of the things that just astounded me with this process is that if you take the advice of people who know what they're doing, they lose weight slowly, a pound a week, something like that. A pound a week is a tiny amount; it's almost imperceptible. Scales can barely measure that accurately and your weight varies by two or three pounds almost every day. So in a week you can't really measure whether you lost a pound. You can only tell every few weeks whether you're on track. That feels really, really slow, but a pound a week for a year is fifty-two pounds. That's nearly four stones of weight. That's a huge amount. So in the short term, the little efforts take just a little bit of time and are perfectly achievable, but they really add up over the long term if you can sustain them. What works in marketing is the same thing that works in school - spaced repetition. It's much better to be seen by someone once a week over eight weeks than it is to be seen eight times on the same day because they only really remember you once or twice from the same day, whereas eight times over eight weeks allows them to remember eight distinct times and it feels like they know you more.

Suzi: If you think you're too busy for all this, and hear yourself thinking, "I can't possibly add anything else into my overly booked schedule. I'm overwhelmed. Who has time for any of this?" Then I'd challenge you to notice that there's plenty of time that you're not aware of that could be allocated towards these activities. For example, do you ever sit and wait for a doctor in a doctor's office? Do you ever stand in a line anywhere? Are you ever sitting in an airport waiting for a plane? Do you ever get to a meeting early and have to wait for the person that you're meeting? That's really all you need. Instead of playing games or checking emails on your handheld device, you can create a blog post, reach out on social media, outline your next article, or make a phone call to reconnect with a past client. It's really a matter of being aware of the time that you have that you are currently not thinking about using for business development or market awareness.

Ian: There are lots of activities that give you fifteen free minutes. I noticed this with myself in taxis. I used to jump into a taxi in London to go somewhere and I would take the time to relax and think about things. But over time I found myself getting out my iPhone and surfing the Web or checking email when that was not really necessary. All of that would have been subsumed into checking email properly when I got back to work at the end of the day. But what I lost is the fifteen minutes of thinking and planning time because it was getting consumed by mindless activities that weren't adding much value yet made me feel as if I was doing work. I think that's what a lot of us do. We do things that feel a bit like work but aren't really. We need to clarify what our priorities really are in order to use our spare fifteen minutes properly.

Getting Support So You Can Build Your Business

Suzi: If you really don't have time (or don't want to make the time) to handle the areas of your business that are not your strengths, or that you just don't like, or they're not the best use of your talents, you can get support and help. You want to find the things that are the best use of you and then outsource everything that is not the best use of you. If you don't care about social media and don't want to be checking Twitter and FaceBook and posting on LinkedIn, then you can hire a virtual assistant to be your social media presence, posting in your "voice" and sharing your content. You can hire a bookkeeper if the best use of you is not keeping all the records straight. You can hire someone (or use software) to track your business development efforts if you're not good at the tracking piece of it. If you don't want to make calls to set appointments, you can hire someone to do that for you or you can get an intern to do it for you and not have to pay as much as you would a virtual assistant. In addition to people that you can hire to help, there are also some automated back office systems that can help as well. There are lots of ways to begin to be strategic about what you're doing even if you're not the one physically doing everything.

Ian: Many coaches resist spending $50 a month on the accounting system or a few hundred dollars a month on virtual assistants to make calls and do social media. They feel like they can't afford it. But the truth is if you put a value on your time, you'll see that you can. Early on you have time to do things yourself because you're not doing so much client work. But once you start getting client work and you need to do your ongoing marketing and business development, your time becomes very, very valuable.

Suzi: I understand when you're just starting out it seems you don't have money to hire help; that the cost issue is a very real one, but there is a point at which you're generating enough revenue that you can afford to hire someone to help you. Prior to that you can be really creative. You can do some bartering with a virtual assistant. Coach them on growing their business in exchange for a certain number of hours of their virtual assistance. Or perhaps there are colleagues you could exchange services or collaborate with to help each of you grow your respective businesses. There are a lot of options that do not cost money, but they take a bit of creativity. Once you're past the start-up point, though, it's important to recognize in any business the time comes when it's not saving you any money to do it yourself. If you're charging $500 an hour as an executive coach, then spending $40 an hour for a virtual assistant is worth the time and investment because it frees you up to be billable for that time as opposed to the cost to you for spending an hour at your billable rate looking at it. Furthermore, though it would take you an hour, it would probably only take your virtual assistant fifteen minutes. You can, of course, figure out how to do webinar technology if you've never done it before. But why not have someone who already knows how to do it set it up for you?

Ian: In fact if they're $40 an hour and you're $500, even if you can do it faster than them and are better than them, it's still worth using them because they've got more time available for that amount of money even if they take twice as long at $40 per hour.

Suzi: Just something to watch out for: As coaches we want to help people develop and we want to be fair and compassionate with people, but if you have a virtual assistant who is not helping, don't remain in that discomfort for very long. It's okay to move on and find another virtual assistant. As coaches we like to be loyal and create long-term relationships, but if you aren't getting the help you need, give yourself the freedom to go elsewhere. An assistant should free you up rather than be needy of your coaching and teaching and training.

Ian: That's true. I have a friend whose assistant started missing appointments for him. She wasn't putting potential client appointments in the diary properly. Obviously you go through all this effort of doing marketing and then if you drop 10 percent of them because of administrative errors, that's a big problem. You just have to bite the bullet and first tell them what they're not doing that you need them to do. But if they can't do it, that's the nature of virtual assistant work, they'll find other people who need the skills they do have and you should find someone that has the skills that you need.

Suzi: There are also some businesses that have cropped up that are essentially brokers for virtual assistants so you can interact with one person who does the legwork for you. You let them know what you're looking for and they will find someone who matches your needs and even manage that person for you. That allows you to create an arm's-length distance between you and the assistant, and if your assistant isn't working out, you can specify the issue to the broker and ask for a new assistant.

Ian: Some virtual assistants are beginning to specialize, and there are some who have lots of experience in working with executive coaches and already know the things you're going to need. Coaches can use virtual assistants to support the mechanics of their marketing, set appointments with executives, phone ahead if you're running late, do your billing, manage your diary, or prepare your presentations or handle your social media.

Suzi: Find what works for you and think about how to be systematic and sustainable around growing your business. Using the coach approach means you don't have to do it all yourself. There are other people who can be part of your community to help you grow your business. There are people you can hire. There are systems you can put in place. It's just a matter of thinking about it in a way that it's going to be sustainable and predictable so you don't have those peaks and valleys. It's about the ongoing activities and mindsets that will allow you to grow your business.

Toolbox

Methods for Marketing While Delivering Services

A common challenge executive coaches face is how to sustainably and systematically grow your business while you are billing time and delivering services to your clients. This checklist of marketing tasks provides activities you can do during your client work to set up an influx of future work, thus eliminating the annoying peaks and valleys of service work.

- Establish a baseline of excellence, delivering great work and exceeding customer expectations.
- Communicate transparently and mindfully.
- Prepare the ground for referrals; plant seeds and request introductions up front.
- Build in "lessons learned" discussions to discuss further work
  - Request testimonials, or take notes when clients praise your work to capture endorsements.
  - When they compliment your work, ask who else they know who would benefit from the same value.
  - Watch and listen for opportunities in their organization throughout your work, and ask about those opportunities during the lessons learned conversation.
- Extend your relationships into the client's organization through key stakeholders.
- Build into your process opportunities to access others in the organization (i.e., feedback interviews).
- Seek different ways to add value beyond what's been contracted.
- Keep your eyes and ears open for opportunities to explore or suggest further work.
- Work on your pipeline of new work all the time, especially while you're still working with a client, not waiting until afterwards.
- Cultivate a mindset of ongoing business development.
- Continue to build the relationship as you wrap up the business
- Find ways to add value to clients after you've finished working together:
  - Send an article or video link that you think will resonate with them
  - Set up a system to notify you of news that's relevant to their company (Google Alerts)

- o Extend empathy and care,
- o Systematically create ways to follow up
- o Reach out and connect
- Turn ongoing contact nurturing into a repeatable system:
  - o Make sure you follow up and keep in touch and add value with a personal element.
  - o Perhaps, if appropriate, add them to your newsletter list.
  - o Put a note in your calendar or CRM.
  - o Set up alerts and reminders for yourself to stay in touch.
  - o Track what you're doing.
  - o Assess what's working.
  - o What's your personal way of staying connected, and how will you track it?
- Make time for marketing: stay active, and plan time in your calendar to keep making contact with potential clients.
- Track how many new people you're meeting and how many are turning into conversations about potentially working together.
- Build time into your model for non-billable time spent cultivating new contacts.
- Build your market presence:
  - o Social media
  - o Writing articles
  - o Blog posts
  - o Answer other blogs
  - o Comment on LinkedIn groups
  - o Update your website
  - o Explore visibility mechanisms
  - o Create videos
  - o Webinars
  - o Presentations
  - o Books
  - o Products,
  - o Branding
  - o PR
  - o Creating assets for your business
- Face to face is the fastest, most secure method to leverage personal relationships and get referrals. It allows for the personal touch and promotes

credibility. But eventually you'll be so billable that you'll need to rely on your business assets to bring people to you.

- Find what works for you - a portfolio of approaches.
  - Refer back to the Marketing Menu.
  - Balance your skills and preferences.
  - Think strategically about what will work for you.
  - Extraverts may want more interpersonal time,
  - Introverts may naturally want more social media, computer time.
  - Honor your frame of reference, but balance internal and external activities.
  - Cultivate your visibility and presence.
- Track your marketing activities and their effectiveness. How much time is it taking you to go to networking events or answer questions on LinkedIn groups? Ask people where they heard of you. Learn what's working for you as to the sources new clients come in through.
- Market presence is small and consistent actions taken over time to drive your visibility and create a cumulative effect, intentionally being findable online and with your target markets.
- Reclaim unconsciously wasted time: waiting in line, at an airport, at the doctor's office, for a meeting to start, sitting in a taxi. Reallocate that time to writing blog posts, updating a social media network, outlining your next article, or calling a past client. Don't confuse activity with progress. Much of your marketing can be done in fifteen minutes or less.
- Get support and help if you don't have time to get marketing handled. Find what's the best use of you and outsource the rest.
  - Hire a virtual assistant to be your social media presence.
  - Hire someone to track your business development efforts for you.
  - Hire an intern to make calls for you.
  - Be strategic about what you're doing even if you're not doing it yourself.
  - Barter if costs are an issue.
  - Team up with colleagues who have complementary skills.
  - Recognize the point at which it's not saving you any money to do it yourself.

What's Next?

Throughout this book we've shared our experiences of the most effective methods for executive coaches to find, connect with, and win clients. Now it's your turn to put what you've learned into action.

As we said back in Chapter 1, how you approach this book will differ depending on your experience and background as a coach. The same goes for how you should approach implementing what you've learned in this book.

- If you're **thinking about becoming a coach** but haven't made the leap yet, your next step is to find out whether coaching is right for you. We recommend using the informational interview approach from Chapter 4 to get a feel for how and who you'd like to coach. It's also a great way to start building your network for when you need it.

- If you're a **newly trained coach,** you should have gone through the whole book step-by-step, paying special attention to the fundamentals of understanding the Bowtie Model and the "mathematics" of winning clients, along with building your understanding of your ideal clients and what they're looking for when hiring a coach. Your most important next step is to start building your contact network using the "coach approach" outlined in Chapter 5.

- If you're already active as a coach, but in your **first year or so of coaching,** you should have looked at all the elements in the book and compared them to your own business model, looking for areas you could improve based on the results you're seeking. You should also be able to run your own numbers through the bowtie model to ensure your marketing system is bringing in the right numbers of the right people to hit your goals. Your next step is to look at how you can improve your system in the areas where you have gaps or "leaks."

- If you're an **established coach,** you've probably skimmed the book with a view to picking up tips and things you can tweak to get better results. Your next step is to make (and keep making) those tweaks. And if you find yourself at any time in the future with fewer clients than you'd like, review your marketing more thoroughly to see whether you've dipped into some bad habits or whether there are bigger areas that could be improved.

- Finally, if you're a **seasoned master coach** you've probably focused mainly on the sections on building sustainability into your business and growing while working with clients. Of course, you'll also want to make sure you continue to excel at the fundamentals, so scheduling time for your own audit of your business development system will allow you to make adjustments and refinements as your success soars.

In each case, turn your notes from the book about what you need to improve or focus on into an action plan. Many of the activities are things you can do quite quickly in the next few weeks. Others are things you'll want to start now and turn into a regular marketing habit or system you'll do on an ongoing basis.

Everything, of course, is dependent on you **taking action**.

If you'd like free access to the electronic copies of the tools from this book along with other resources to help you win more coaching clients, then you can register for free at the Executive Coach Marketing Resource Center here: http://libraryofprofessionalcoaching.com/marketing/executive-coach-marketing-resource-centre/.

We wish you every success with your marketing. This book has shown you the fundamentals that every coach needs to win coaching clients. Now, it's up to you. Get out there and leverage an executive coach approach to marketing!

About the Authors:

About Ian Brodie

Ian Brodie is a marketing specialist who works exclusively with coaches and other professionals to help them win more clients.

He's sold multimillion dollar engagements around the world and worked in seventeen different countries. *Top Sales World Magazine* listed him as one of the top fifty global thought leaders in marketing and sales, *OpenView Labs* say he's one of the top sales influencers in the world, and *RainToday* named his website as one of the "resources of the decade" for professional services marketing.

But in truth, Ian says he's far from a natural salesperson – in fact it was something of a nasty surprise to him when he realized early on in his career that in order to progress and do the kind of work he was interested in, he would need to learn to sell. But through study, experience, and having some of the best "rainmakers" in the field as his mentors, he's learned what it takes for even the most reluctant of professionals to become highly effective at marketing and sales – and that's what he teaches his clients today.

His particular focus these days is on working with small firms and solo professionals. Since leaving the corporate world many years ago he's been astounded at the depth of talent and passion for clients in the small and solo businesses he's met. Yet he's also seen how many of these businesses are struggling or failing to live up to their potential simply because they haven't "cracked" marketing and selling.

He's made it his mission to help sole practitioners and small firms escape from being the "best kept secret" in their field and to get the clients, recognition and rewards they deserve.

On a personal note, he's married to the wonderful Kathy, and they have two grown-up children – Chris & Robs.

http://www.ianbrodie.com

About Suzi Pomerantz

Suzi Pomerantz, CEO of Innovative Leadership International, LLC is an award-winning executive coach and #1 bestselling author with 22 years experience coaching leaders and teams in over 200 organizations.

Suzi specializes in leadership influence, helping executives and organizations find clarity in chaos.

She was among the first awarded the Master credential from the ICF 17 years ago and is a thought leader serving on several Boards. She served on the IJCO Editorial Board, the ICCO Advisory Board, the International Executive Coaching Summit board, the *Harvard Business Review* Advisory Council.

She has authored over 30 publications about coaching, ethics, and business development, and has authored or co-authored 9 books including her bestseller, ***Seal the Deal*** and the #1 international bestseller *Ready, Aim, Captivate*, co-authored with Deepak Chopra and other luminaries.

Suzi designed the LEAP Tiered Coaching Program for leadership teams, founded the Leading Coaches' Center and co-founded the Library of Professional Coaching: the world's largest free online library for coaches.

In 2013, Suzi was inducted into Bestselling Authors International Organization. In 2014, she was invited to become the Director of Training for the Leadership Coaching and Organizational Performance program at George Mason University and Rutgers University. In 2015, Suzi was invited to join the Association for Coaching Excellence.

On a personal note, she has been married to Bruce for 17 years and they have two children in middle school.

http://www.InnovativeLeader.com

Executive Coach Marketing Resource Centre:

We've created a resource center for the book at the Library of Professional Coaching here:

http://libraryofprofessionalcoaching.com/marketing/executive-coach-marketing-resource-centre/

The resource center contains all the checklists and workbooks from the book, along with links to other useful resources to help you get results from your marketing fast.